Gh[osts]
a beginner's guide

TERESA MOOREY

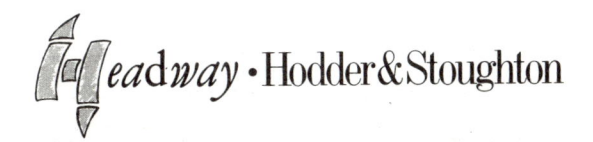

Headway · Hodder & Stoughton

For Jonathan

Acknowledgements

Thanks to Michael Roll for supplying so much information. As always, thanks to my friend Jane Brideson, for being there to discuss my ideas, and for illustrating the books.

Order queries: please contact Bookpoint Ltd, 39 Milton Park, Abingdon, Oxon OX14 4TD. Telephone: (44) 01235 400414, Fax: (44) 01235 400454. Lines are open from 9.00–6.00, Monday to Saturday, with a 24 hour message answering service. Email address: orders@bookpoint.co.uk

A catalogue record for this title is available from The British Library

ISBN 0 340 73064 1

First published 1998
Impression number   10 9 8 7 6 5 4 3 2 1
Year   2003 2002 2001 2000 1999 1998

Copyright © 1998 Teresa Moorey

All rights reserved. No part of this publication may be reproduced or transmitted in any form or by any means, electronic or mechanical, including photocopy, recording, or any information storage and retrieval system, without permission in writing from the publisher or under licence from the Copyright Licensing Agency Limited. Further details of such licences (for reprographic reproduction) may be obtained from the Copyright Licensing Agency Limited, of 90 Tottenham Court Road, London, W1P 9HE.

Typeset by Transet Limited, Coventry, England.
Printed in Great Britain for Hodder & Stoughton Educational, a division of Hodder Headline plc, 338 Euston Road, London NW1 3BH by Cox and Wyman Limited, Reading, Berks.

CONTENTS

Introduction	1
Chapter 1 What is a Ghost?	2
Different types of ghosts	3
Hauntings	4
Revenants	6
Ghouls	7
Poltergeists	11
Phantoms of the living	12
Vampires	16
Science and the ether	18
Chapter 2 Ouija and thought forms	21
The 'ladder of selves'	23
Entities	24
Personal experience	27
Thought forms	30
Chapter 3 Attitudes to death	38
Native attitudes to death	38
Tibetan beliefs	41
Modern beliefs	43
Out-of-body experience	44
Near-death experience	46
Hallowe'en	48

Chapter 4 Scientific proof of survival after death — 52

- Mediumship — 53
- Ideas and opinions — 57
- Historical case studies — 59
- A science of survival — 60

Chapter 5 Coping with phenomena — 65

- The commonplace — 67
- Malevolent encounters — 68
- Exorcism — 73
- If you are haunted … — 74
- Strengthening yourself — 75
- Cleansing — 77
- Protecting yourself — 78
- Cleansing your living area — 80

Further reading and resources — 83

INTRODUCTION

Do you believe in ghosts? This is not a simple question to answer; a 'ghost' may not be easy to define and, until we are sure what we mean, how can we say whether we believe in ghosts or not? Usually, by 'ghost' we mean the spirit of a dead person, but there are other possibilities. Perhaps ghosts are impressions left by some means as yet unidentified by science on the surroundings, which have no life of their own. Perhaps they are manifestations of energies within a person or the earth. They may be malevolent entities out to cause trouble. Or they may be something else entirely. Some will say that all ghostly happenings are pure imagination; however, strange happenings, hauntings and apparitions are so common that many people have some tale to tell. Surely to dismiss all such phenomena as non-existent, pure fantasy, is somewhat sweeping?

Ghosts can be a problem. What do you do if you hear footsteps when you know you are alone in the house, or sense an atmosphere, or feel a 'cold spot' or actually see the shape of a previous occupant of the place, now deceased? Do you tell yourself this is 'just imagination'? Some people find this laughable; some walk with a constant semi-perception of the spirit world at the corner of their eye. There are more things in heaven and earth …

Perhaps a more open, pragmatic and practical approach is called for. Perhaps we should avoid scorn and the presuppositions of our materialistic culture and try to overcome our fears to take a common-sense look at these phenomena. If you are interested in what is hidden, unexplored or mysterious, or if you have had experiences that you have not been able to explain, you may like to consider and investigate the world of ghosts.

1 WHAT IS A GHOST?

What beckoning ghost along the moonlight shade
Invites my steps, and points to yonder glade.

Alexander Pope, *Elegy to the Memory of an Unfortunate Lady*

Ghost stories are as old as humanity. Cultures worldwide repeat the theme of spirits of the dead coming back to haunt the living and most, if not all, belief systems include doctrines about existence beyond the grave. Stories about ghosts never fail to fascinate, generating shivers of fear and delight. Ghosts rarely cause any physical harm to those they visit, but we fear the unknown and we fear death, and ghosts combine both elements. However, ghosts also give us hope of enduring consciousness after the dissolution of the physical body. At the heart of the mystery of ghosts lies the universal question 'Are we eternal?'

While denial of the afterlife was regarded as heresy in medieval Europe, actual communication with spirits lent itself to a dangerous charge of witchcraft. The 'Age of Reason' followed with the idea of a 'clockwork universe' in which ghosts held questionable place. However, in the nineteenth century interest in psychic phenomena returned in a more sympathetic environment, leading to the foundation of the Society for Psychical Research in 1882, in London. Its membership included many highly educated and eminent persons, such as Alfred Lord Tennyson, William Gladstone and Lewis Carroll.

A study carried out in the late nineteenth century called the 'Census of Hallucinations', indicated that more than one million adult Victorians had seen or heard a ghost. A more recent British survey revealed that 44 per cent of the population believe in ghosts and, of these, one in seven claim to have seen a ghost or to have been haunted. In the United States the figures are even higher; studies have shown that 57 per cent of adults believe in ghosts. There are so many accounts of ghosts that to assert they do not exist, at least in some form, would seem to fly in the face of the evidence.

Different Types of Ghosts

Mediums and those interested in the occult have always believed in ghosts. However, whatever may be behind ghostly phenomena, and however they may materialise, not all ghosts are the same. Ghosts can manifest in many different ways: some are felt as 'cold spots' where the temperature appears to plummet and an icy current is felt around the ankles; some manifest as an atmosphere, a feeling of unease or oppression, but also sometimes of gladness and peace; others are heard as 'things that go bump in the night'; some are active, switching on electrical objects and moving furniture; many manifest as bad smells or pleasant scents. Ghosts also literally touch people, and while there can be few things more terrifying than the brush of unseen fingers on the back of the neck, many a bereaved person has been comforted by the gentle touch of a loved one, carrying their own special, recognisable signature. The most spectacular ghost stories are always visual, however. Pale ladies in medieval dress and headless cavaliers have been seen by many people. But these are varieties of manifestation. Behind them lie different types of ghostly agency.

Hauntings

The classic type of ghost is indeed a spirit of one departed, yet earthbound, held in bondage to their old existence because of trauma, strong emotion or similar. Such a ghost has a consciousness of its own. When alive (in the scientific sense) we do not just possess a material body, but we also have several other 'subtle' bodies that interpenetrate the physical one, existing in the same space as the material body. This ancient belief may be becoming reconciled to science with the discovery of 'quarks' which are sub-atomic particles that vibrate at great speed and can pass straight through solid objects. Indeed, physics has taught us for many years that matter is mostly empty space with atoms composed of electrons and nuclei, separated from each other by vast distances. Yet we do not experience the world in this way – it seems solid, presumably because our physical body vibrates at the same rate as our surroundings. Our subtle body, on the other hand, vibrates at different rates, which is why it is able to occupy the same space as the physical. The closest subtle body to the physical is often called the astral body and this is connected to the physical body by the etheric, or energy body. The energy centres, known as the chakras, are organs in the etheric body, marking its points of strongest connection to the physical. The chakras are described and explored in *The Wheel of the Year – Myth and Magic Through the Seasons* and *Witchcraft – a beginner's guide* in this series, and are explained in detail in *Chakras for beginners* also in this series.

When we die it seems we pass out of our physical body into the etheric body. Occultists teach that this is attached to the physical body by a silver thread, arising from the head or the abdomen and visible to some psychics. When we sleep we may travel in our dreams in our astral body, but the silver cord remains intact. At

what is a ghost?

death it is severed and the soul is free. However, some people remain trapped in their etheric body, instead of moving on to other realms. The etheric is designed to form a bridge between the physical and the spirit bodies, but when consciousness gets stuck in the etheric, without a physical body, everything becomes diffuse, confusing and cloudy. Such ghosts have little idea of time. To them a hundred years may seem as one. They may also be unaware of other ghosts haunting the same physical space. They inhabit a kind of limbo, an existence leading nowhere. Because for them this is sad and confusing, it is no wonder that many ghosts create a disturbing atmosphere.

One experience I had of this sort of ghost certainly seemed to emphasise the pathos possible in such situations. It took place in the house of a friend of a friend, whom I occasionally visited. For some reason I hated going to the lavatory in the bathroom of this house and would put it off until I was desperate. When it was dark I felt especially uneasy, panicking when I could not find the light switch. I felt most un-private, convinced that someone was watching me.

I could not take my eyes off the bath, for some reason, as if I feared to be taken by surprise from there, although all that I could see was usually the clothes airer!

Eventually, I told my hostess of my fears. 'Oh,' she replied, 'it must be Terry'. Terry, I knew, was her former husband. I realised that the marriage had been unhappy, but we hadn't talked about the details and I had assumed they were divorced. However, it now transpired that Terry was dead. In fact, he had been electrocuted in the bath, having attempted some amateur rewiring. His widow, far from mourning him, had been glad he had died, for he was abusive and violent and she was pleased to be rid of him. There is a farcical element to this – being electrocuted in one's bath and lingering as a confused voyeur of other people's private moments. Terry may well have wondered why everyone was so ready to relieve themselves or take their clothes off in his presence! However, I felt quite upset by the whole affair and even more reluctant to go to the bathroom.

One day, at my friend's house, I found myself crying as if my heart was broken, and yet I did not know why – it was an odd feeling, as if it was not really me who was crying, although the tears were pouring down my cheeks. Then I found myself saying 'He's sorry, he says he's so sorry. He didn't mean any of it and he wants you to forgive him.' As it turned out, this was the anniversary of Terry's death. His widow wasn't especially impressed, not because she did not believe me, for she had an interest in such matters, but because she could not bring herself to forgive Terry or take his sorrow seriously. This I found even more upsetting, because I felt that Terry could not make his peace and move on unless she accepted his apology. Of course, this story could be interpreted in different ways and it could all be put down to my imagination. However, it didn't feel like that to me.

Revenants

The term 'revenant' is derived from the French word *revenir*, to come back. A revenant is a ghost that has a consciousness of its own, however, in this case it is not trapped but comes back by choice, probably because of something pleasant. The revenant literally returns from the spirit world to visit old 'haunts'. Those who experience a revenant may find it difficult to distinguish from a haunting, but there is much more likely to be an atmosphere of gladness.

Lady Caroline Lamb, sexy socialite and lover of Lord Byron, is said to haunt the In and Out club in London, where she dazzled and flirted at many parties. Apparently she is a revenant, not a trapped spirit. However, when we die we do not automatically become all-wise, and while we may be at peace and open-minded enough to pass on to spirit realms, we may still be preoccupied with the essentially trivial. While a revenant may be a basically non-threatening visitation, it does seem that such spirits have not effectively moved on, or found a way to progress, if they are continually drawn back to scenes of earthly triumphs.

Ghouls

A ghoul is, strictly speaking, a ghastly fiend that preys on dead flesh, and we use the term to describe anyone who has an appetite for the gruesome. However, a different definition of 'ghoul' was developed by the archaeologist and dowser, Tom Lethbridge. Lethbridge is well-known for his experiments in dowsing in relation to the paranormal, but here we are concerned with his theory of ghouls.

In 1924, while at Choristers' School, Lethbridge and a friend heard a master remark 'The ghoul is on the stairs again'. The master looked deeply depressed and so the pair went off to investigate for themselves, finding a strange, unpleasant presence at the bottom of the staircase. Lethbridge described it as icy, but more than that it was full of misery. Lethbridge and his friend 'pushed' the ghoul before them all the way up the stairs, when it reappeared behind them. They then pushed it back downstairs once more. Later the school was exorcised, resulting in the retreat of the ghoul into a bathroom and subsequently into an external passageway where the servants left their bikes.

Another similar experience happened when Lethbridge was eighteen as he and his mother were walking through the Great Wood near Wokingham in Surrey, England. At the same moment, and quite out of the blue, they both experienced an acute depression. Some days later they found that the body of a suicide had been discovered close to the spot where they had encountered the feeling of gloom. The most notable experience, however, happened to Lethbridge and his wife at Ladram Bay in Dorset, England, where they were both overcome by a feeling of terrible depression. This was endorsed by other family members on separate occasions. Lethbridge described the feeling as similar to the feeling experienced when running a temperature and full of medication, tingling and giddiness. Lethbridge's wife went to the clifftop and had the horrid impression that someone was urging her to jump.

Dowsers may experience a tingling feeling when they detect water, and as the 'ghouls' had all manifested near a watercourse or in damp, muggy conditions, this led Lethbridge to the theory that water acts in a way similar to a photographic film, recording the emotions of those nearby, especially if the emotions are strong. Lethbridge went on to speculate that the Greek idea of naiads, dryads and nereids, spirits of water, wood and sea respectively, were personifications of the natural, but unrecognised effects of the water, acting as a field upon which strong emotions were imprinted. Thus the feelings of the man who committed suicide would have been impressed upon the dryad-field nearby. Trees always have water close, held within them and often flowing nearby or underground. Other accounts of similar phenomena describe the appearance of greyish light, a feeling of fathomless evil and a terrible sensation of being drained of all energy.

Lethbridge's theories are recorded in several of his books, mentioned in Further Reading. In *Mysteries* (also listed in Further Reading) Colin Wilson expands the ghoul theory, as follows:

> *Could it be that 'negative emotions' – like fear and misery – record themselves by draining energy from a magnetic field; and when someone 'tunes in' to the recording, it has the effect of stealing his energies and blurring his faculties? Dr Arthur Guirdham, Chief Psychiatric Consultant to the Bath Medical Area, has stated that*

he knows several houses in Bath that have a history of mental illness and suicide; that is, where one tenant after another has become ill with depression ... When patients were removed from these houses, the depression promptly vanished ....

It is quite conceivable that prolonged exposure to a draining atmosphere could result in mental disturbance. Not all ghoulish visitations can be explained as 'recordings', however. Lethbridge himself encountered something more active on Skellig Michael, an island off the coast of Kerry in 1924. Descending a cliff to investigate a rubbish-dump below he felt convinced that someone was wanting to push him off the cliff, and this feeling became so strong that he decided to abandon his attempt. A short time later, walking down the low hill below the ruins of an eighth-century monastery, he felt that he must turn around, but before he was able to do so, something knocked him to the ground. When he got up, the countryside was deserted.

Similar phenomena have been recorded as far apart as Ealing, in London and Oklawaha, Florida. Andrew Green, an active investigator of hauntings, visited a house in Montpellier Road, Ealing, where three people had died having fallen from the tower, and when Green stood there he also felt a strange urge to jump. The house at Oklawaha was the scene where the notorious Ma Baker and her son Freddie were shot dead, in 1935. This is haunted by footfalls and quarrelling voices, quite possibly because of the atmosphere of violence and tension that must have preceded the deaths – the Ma Baker house stands on the banks of Lake Weir, so supporting the theory that such events are connected with nearby water.

It seems likely that strong feelings do leave their imprint behind. Happy feelings can also linger. In *Ghosthunter* (see Further Reading) Eddie Burks describes a psychic imprint he sensed at the RAF base at Linton-on-Ouse, North Yorkshire, England. In this base, scene of several hauntings, there was one corridor where the cleaner felt like singing. Eddie was conscious of great joy and excitement. Eddie, who is a psychic talented at laying ghosts to rest, 'made contact' and told of a pilot who had been reported dead towards the end of the Second World War. His grieving wife had given up hope of ever seeing him again. Several days later she was informed that he had, in fact, arrived safely back at the base and was being debriefed. Full of joy she rushed up to the base and ran down the corridor to embrace him. This incident had been so highly charged that it had left behind its 'imprint' but no consciousness was involved; in fact, the two people might still be alive.

So is a ghoul merely a 'psychic imprint'? Sometimes, perhaps, but I doubt whether this is always the case. The type of ghoul that depresses and sucks energy may possess a type of consciousness, simply finding it easier to manifest under certain conditions such as the presence of water underground or in the atmosphere. Destructive envy is not unusual, and it is all too common to find individuals who want to destroy what others possess if they cannot have it themselves, while alive. This process may be even more powerful when unconscious. There also exist twisted souls who enjoy upsetting and frightening others, because it is their only means to feel powerful. If we believe in survival after death, there is no reason why these impulses should die with the physical body, and so a 'ghoul' may be an earthbound spirit, chained to some nasty habits acquired in life as the only means to satisfaction.

However, a disturbing theory also exists that there are non-human agencies that feed on the energies given off by fear – an idea explored in *The Dark Gods* by Anthony Roberts and Geoff Gilbertson (Panther, 1985). Occultists confirm that the greatest releases of energy occur with sex and at death, and killing of animals is still employed by some unscrupulous people as part of rituals. Some have reported that the ancient Egyptians created thought forms to protect the pyramids by torturing slaves to death and using their pain, fear and rage to create a malevolent entity to protect the tomb. Whatever one believes – and I doubt the Egyptians were so crude and cruel – if there are entities that feed off fear and the energy release at death, they might conceivably hang around certain localities urging humans to suicide, so they can 'feed'. Far-fetched? Yes, I agree. However, there is often substance to age-old beliefs, and here we are chillingly close to the original idea of a 'demon that feeds off the dead'.

Poltergeists

The literal meaning of 'poltergeist' is 'noisy spirit'. Poltergeist activity involves many different phenomena of a physical nature. Heavy furniture may be moved, household objects float through the air, all sorts of knockings, bangs and gabbling voices may be heard, objects go missing and reappear in odd places, crockery is smashed, written messages appear, stones shower down and, in the worst visitations, there is a great deal of destruction and annoyance. Often the 'spirit' seems mischievous and to have a pronounced sense of humour.

Of all ghostly and related phenomena, poltergeists are the best established and documented, so much so that the fact that something is indeed going on is rarely disputed, even by the most sceptical. There are accounts of poltergeists from all over the world. The earliest documented case dates as far back as 530 CE (Common Era), when a deacon Helpidius of Ravenna in Italy was afflicted by a shower of stones. St Caesarius banished the phenomenon by sprinkling the house with holy water.

A more recent and most notable, documented in *Modern Mysteries of Britain* (see Further Reading), case occurred in Reading, Berkshire, England, in 1979, and lasted for eighteen months. The two unfortunate folk involved were Mrs Adams, a lady in her eighties, and her daughter Pauline, who was fifty. Large objects were moved and several TV sets destroyed – this was an especially destructive spirit. All the household crockery was smashed and holiday savings of £50 were shredded. Mrs Adams' seventeen-year-old grandson was standing in the living room one day when all his clothes simply flew off, leaving him in his underpants. So they asked the 'spirit' to return the clothes, and they rematerialised one by one on top of the door. The young man had to unbutton the shirt and unlace his shoes before putting them back on, for they reappeared fastened in just the way he had been wearing them. Unlike most poltergeists that are merely frightening, the Reading manifestation did cause several injuries, the worst being an injury to Mrs Adams' head, when her small pill-box struck her, resulting in her needing two stitches. A priest was called to perform an exorcism, but this was only temporarily successful and the phenomenon returned, despite attempts by several mediums to help, and the family finally moved house to escape.

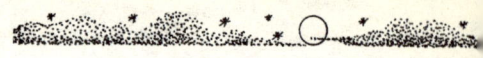

Poltergeists are sometimes dismissed as the work of mischievous children, and while this may account for some cases, it cannot explain all of them. Perhaps the most popular theory regarding the nature of poltergeists is that they are, in fact, the product of an unconscious emanation of energy from one of the people involved. Often, this may be a teenager on the threshold of puberty, and the phenomena subside spontaneously in time, presumably when the person concerned has passed through the turbulent emotional phase. It may be that poltergeists arise from suppression and inhibition of strong feelings, especially at times of hormonal change when passions and desires may run high. This seems like a reasonable theory, although it does not explain the mechanics of floating cups and saucers.

Phantoms of the Living

One of the most chilling incidents to my knowledge concerned a friend of my mother's. This is what happened.

The friend, who we will call Dorothy, had been having vivid dreams in which the same cottage appeared all the time. In her dream she would approach the cottage, alongside a wall covered with clambering dog-roses. A paved path, flanked with lavender, led to the front door which was made of solid wood, warped and seasoned by time, with a diamond-shaped window pane in the centre. Dorothy would go up this path, brushing the lavender with her skirt as she went. The old door would open to her touch, leading to a hallway with parquet flooring, redolent of polish. From there she would move into the sunny kitchen. Yellow curtains opened on a window that displayed a garden stocked with herbs and flowers. Dorothy had been a city dweller for most of her life, so this cottage was her dream home in more ways than one.

One day, while holidaying in the West Country of England with her mother, Dorothy was driving slowly, to relax and absorb the picturesque countryside. Rounding a bend, she suddenly had the strangest feeling. This place was familiar, although she had never in her life visited this part of the country before. It was lucky that hers was the only car on the road, for she stopped abruptly, all the hairs on the back of her neck standing on end. There, surely, was the wall covered in dog-roses that she knew so well from her dream. She got out of the car and walked beside the wall until, sure enough, there was the gate and the path with lavender stems overhanging the paving stones. Bemused, she walked down the path, as she had so many times in her dreams, and, peering through the diamond pane, she knocked on the door. It was opened by a faded, middle-aged woman, who looked at Dorothy and took a faltering step backwards, her face as white as parchment.

Dorothy was far too excited to take much notice of the woman's reaction. Words tumbled out 'I do apologise for bothering you, but I was driving past and I just had to come in – it's so beautiful, but eerie, too, in a way. This really is my dream home. Can I ask you, is it for sale?'

By this time the woman had retreated back into the hallway, which smelt of new polish on the parquet floor. She was leaning on the mahogany hall-stand – also familiar to Dorothy – for support.

'N-no, I mean, yes, possibly, but ...'

'This really is uncanny,' Dorothy went on, looking about her in wonderment. 'I know this house so well. If it is for sale I really am very interested.'

'Oh, you wouldn't want to buy this place, I don't think. I shouldn't think anyone would,' the other woman continued.

'But it's lovely, why ever not?' Dorothy asked, now noticing the woman's strange palor and her look of fear.

'Because it's haunted,' came the reply.

'Oh,' said Dorothy, with a smile. She was ever the sceptic when it came to tales of the supernatural. 'Who haunts it, then?'

'Why ... you do,' the woman answered.

I do not know what followed, but as far as I am aware, Dorothy never bought the lovely West Country cottage. It must be a scary feeling indeed to be told that a part of you seems to have gone wandering, without your control, as if you already have one foot in the land beyond the grave.

Something far less dramatic, but similar, happened once to me. At the time I was working in an office job that I truly hated, for I cannot bear routine and found the work boring in the extreme. I really felt as if I was imprisoned from nine to five each day, away from sunlight, books, poetry, stimulating ideas and companionship, with dry documents around me and not a kindred spirit in sight. My private life, too, was frustrating – it seemed there was nowhere I could be 'me'. One day a friend said he had seen me the day before on the sea-front (I lived in Leigh-on-Sea in Essex, England, at the time). Now, I knew quite well that I had been nowhere near the sea and told him so. 'Oh yes,' he insisted, 'it was you, all right. I saw your face clearly, but you were too snooty to speak to me. You were wearing a dark drown skirt and a peachy coloured blouse, and you walked straight past me.' At that point I did get a creepy feeling, because that was what I had been wearing, and he couldn't possibly have known it.

Occultists accept that our astral, or subtle, body can separate from the physical while we sleep, and that many dreams, especially those featuring flying are partially recalled snippets of our astral travelling. Some people are able to astral travel consciously, projecting their consciousness out of their body at will. It seems that Dorothy's experience may simply have been astral travel while sleeping, done repeatedly, and that the person living in the cottage was sensitive enough to see her, on her visits. I am certainly prepared to believe that the intense frustration of my life at the time my friend reported seeing me could have resulted in part of me going wandering in spirit – it was what my heart desired, after all. More recently, one of my sons has told me on several occasions that he has seen me in the house in the morning (he gets up earlier than I do, for his newspaper delivery job) although I am still in bed dozing. When I have been feeling very down he has perceived me as a dark figure – and I must say that it hasn't cheered me up at all to be told about this at breakfast!

Many events such as this, but more spectacular, are well documented. There is a term for a living phantasm – a 'doppelganger'. Possibly the most striking case concerns a French schoolmistress, called Emilie Sagee, who was born in Dijon, in 1813, and lost no less than eighteen jobs in sixteen years because of her disturbing talent for being in two places at once. Her pupils often argued about exactly where she was at a given time. One day the class was amazed to see two Emilies, standing side by side, both writing with chalk on the board! Her 'double' vanished, as she whirled around, startled by the shouts of the class. On another occasion, when Emilie has left the class for a short while to consult the headmistress, she was suddenly perceived sitting in her chair in front of another class. Some of the braver children ventured to touch her and reported that she felt like muslin. One of them walked through her – then the apparition vanished. When Emilie was asked about this, she said that at that moment she had looked in through the window and felt concerned that the class was without a teacher. Some of the pupils who were with the 'real' Emilie noticed that she looked pale and ill at the time that her double appeared. Unfortunately, despite the fact that Emilie was an excellent teacher, she had to be asked to leave because some of the children were upset by her talent. Emilie took up residence with her sister-in-law, and the family became accustomed to her ability to be in two places at once. However, one day Emilie left home and simply vanished.

Emilie lived in an era when young women of a certain class were severely inhibited, resulting sometimes in 'fits of the vapours' and other hysterical behaviour. Possibly Emilie's ability to get 'out of herself' was related in some way to the fact that many of her natural energies, notably sexual ones, were stifled. A similar description would fit me, during my office incarceration. It is a pity that such manifestations inspire fear in those who witness them and are simply disbelieved by those who don't, for here an important human faculty may lie dormant.

Vampires

Vampires are dismissed as morbid Balkan imagination or a product of the Hammer House of Horror. Bram Stoker, in his novel *Dracula* made vampirism famous and even glamorous, and remakes of the Dracula story are still box-office successes. This may be because of the sexual undertones, or even due to the fact that the amount of blood involved betrays a secret fascination with the still partly taboo subject of menstruation, as discussed by Shuttle and Redgrove in *The Wise Wound* (HarperCollins, 1994). 'Vampire' derives from the Slavonic *wampyr* but belief in vampires was equally strong in Britain, and the custom of burying the unhallowed dead at crossroads with a stake through the heart – abolished by law in 1823 – was to prevent the corpse from becoming a vampire.

There are several versions of belief in vampires. One version is that an evil spirit takes up residence in the newly dead body of someone wicked enough to have links with it. Others say that a vampire is an earth-bound soul of an especially nasty kind. This creature clings to earth and prevents its human body from decaying by sending out an etheric double to prey on the lifeblood of others, and so maintain its own unholy existence. In this case it is not so much the blood that is consumed but the vitality of the victim. A third theory holds that it is the physical body that leaves the tomb by night, in search of blood to maintain its hideous life. The Slavs term this thing *Nosferatu*, 'the Undead'.

There are many stories of English vampires of the twelfth century, and lore exists as to what will repel vampires. Garlic is useful for this and the wild dog-rose, *Rosa Canina*. Dogs, which are sensitive to anything sinister, will bark at the approach of the Undead. A 'vampire plague' occurred in Meduegya, Servia (now Serbia), in 1732 – the source, no doubt, of our association of vampires with Transylvania. Doreen Valiente recounts this in *An ABC of Witchcraft, Past and Present* (Hale, 1994).

> ... *a man called Arnod Paole had been killed by falling from a wagon. During his lifetime, Paole often recounted how he had once been bitten by a vampire. The people of Meduegya soon had*

good reason to remember these tales, when an outbreak of vampirism began to terrorise the neighbourhood. As a result of it four people died.

It was decided to open Paole's grave, and forty days after his burial this was done. The body was found to be quite fresh, and shockingly stained with blood. The vampire corpse was burnt at once; but the epidemic continued to spread ... the trouble reached such proportions that it came to the ears of the government, and official action was taken.

A detachment of soldiers, including three army surgeons, together with their commanding officer, were sent to Meduegya. Their orders were to open the graves of those who had died recently, examine the bodies, and, if necessary, burn those which appeared to be in the vampire condition.

They made a detailed report of what they found, dated 7th January 1732. It makes one of the most amazing and grisly stories ever to find its way into official records. Thirteen graves were opened in all; and of these, ten were found to contain corpses that were fresh and rosy-cheeked, and which when dissected proved to contain fresh blood. The other three bodies, although exhumed from the same cemetary, and in some cases more recently interred ... were undergoing the normal process of decomposition.

All the bodies which were found to be in the vampire condition were beheaded and then burnt to ashes.

Of course, we can simply dismiss this chilling account as being somehow the product of the superstition that was rife two-and-a-half centuries ago. Is there a 'rational' explanation? By 'rational' we mean, of course, something that doesn't threaten our cherished beliefs or ask us to reformulate our theories of how the world works. Most of the time these 'theories' seem like unassailable facts and anything that contradicts them is dismissed. It is unlikely that a report of modern vampirism would be taken seriously. How many doctors would consider, even momentarily, the possibility of death caused by vampirism? The death certificate would no doubt display the label 'Death from severe blood loss, of unknown cause' or similar.

I do not claim to believe in vampires. But I do go along with oft-quoted Hamlet that there are 'more things in heaven and earth – and if I ever have to spend a night in a crypt I shall garland myself with garlic and take a rowan stake, just in case! One fact of which we can be more sure, however, is that there exists a type of 'psychic vampire' – a person who, while being very much alive, unconsciously drains the vitality of those around, especially the susceptible, in a real way. Such people are often self-centred and/or obsessively possessive. They may mean no harm, but their presence can be invasive and debilitating in the extreme. Some people also assert that their vitality has been drained by occult means, quite deliberately. Of course, this can be a convenient excuse, but might be possible under certain conditions, particularly with someone whose etheric body had been weakened in some way, perhaps by drugs. If this should be the case, the perpetrator would, in time, find that the practice had rebounded upon them in some way, but meanwhile this would have destructive effects upon the sufferer. Hints will appear later in the book to strengthen psychic protection, generally.

Science and the ether

The prevailing 'rational' view states that ghosts are outside the realms of science and, as such, do not exist. However, the physics of the twenty-first century appear to be approaching the ancient territory of the mystics. The ether is a subtle medium, believed by occultists to permeate all of space. According to the latest theories, empty space is not 'empty' at all, but rather a 'quantum vacuum'. The whole of space is, indeed, filled with a 'zero-point field' in which the particles of matter arise, as 'standing waves'.

The evidence of the Russian physicist Akimov indicates that all objects create vortices in the cosmic ether and these 'torsion waves' can continue even when the objects that generated them are no longer present. Vladimir Poponin and his team of scientists at the Institute of Biochemical Physics of the Russian Academy of Science conducted experiments in this field. A laser beam was directed at a

DNA sample, generating an expected interference pattern. However, this pattern persisted long after the DNA had been removed, creating a 'phantom effect' of a new field structure from the physical vacuum. This phantom effect indicates the existence of a previously overlooked vacuum substructure – the old idea of the 'ether'. If this is the case, we all interact with this substructure and it underlies our evolvement. We are not isolated entities but exist in relation to the rest of creation.

Here the cosmic web begins to enter the realms of science, indicating that we are all part of a mysterious but connected network, and that there are subtle realities that we may affect and which we may sense, leading us towards one theory of what ghosts may be. Ghosts have long been considered by psychics to exist in the ether and, if matter is simply a type of vibration as seems to be the case, ghosts may just be entities of one sort or another, vibrating at a different rate from ourselves, thus visible only under exceptional circumstances. We shall be looking at related themes in a later chapter. However we approach a theory of ghosts, it is reasonable to regard ghosts as established fact, and to proceed on that basis.

PRACTICE – GHOSTHUNTING

If you are interested in ghosts and the supernatural you have probably thought about ghosthunting at some point. It isn't unusual to encounter people who will warn you off this 'dangerous dabbling' – however, many more people are hurt in road accidents than are harmed in any way by the supernatural.

Having said this, it certainly isn't a good idea for any of us to launch ourselves unprepared into the unknown. That sounds like the psychic equivalent of a biker travelling at 100 mph without a crash helmet. It is true that people have encountered some extremely unpleasant things when looking for ghosts and similar phenomena, and on rare occasions these haven't been easy to get rid of. So my word to the wise is to keep away from places that have a bad reputation, that have been associated with nasty rituals, crimes, or are reported to be haunted by something that appears to dislike the living, especially crypts and graveyards.

Ghosthunting needs to be taken seriously and treated with respect. Quite apart from anything else, it is unfair to treat troubled spirits as a floor show.

However, there may be little harm in visiting the houses of friends or trusted acquaintances who report a friendly haunting, in order to experience it for yourself. A friend of my son's, for instance, lives in a haunted house. Regularly the ghost is heard to descend a disused staircase (now used as shelves for books, plants and ornaments), to settle itself comfortably in a wicker armchair. It harms no one, but my son's friend usually asks someone to spend the night with him when his family are away! However, whenever visiting anywhere remotely 'ghostly' it is always best to take steps to protect yourself, as outlined in Chapter 5, for you may be especially sensitive or psychic and the experience could upset you more than you imagine.

Another form of ghosthunting that is harmless, and can be interesting, is to collect local anecdotes and stories. You may discover such things just by asking around, especially if you live in the country, for country people often have a tale to tell. Hotels and old houses quite often claim to have a ghost. The local library may be able to help you. Use your sleuthing skills to locate people who have seen or heard ghosts and interview them – reports may sometimes be found in the local newspaper. You may piece stories together to come up with an interesting picture, or uncover historical facts that support anecdotes.

Good hunting!

2 OUIJA AND THOUGHT FORMS

The departed Spirits are often terrible liars and on no account are you to believe their words.

Emmanuel Swedenborg

'Ouija' is made up of the French word *oui* and the German *ja*, both meaning 'yes'. Ouija is pronounced 'wee-ja' or 'wee-jee'. It is a board bearing an alphabet, often a planchette which is a board mounted in two castors, with a pencil point, which can be used for automatic writing and spirit contact. A simpler version can be constructed using individual letters of the alphabet written on small pieces of card or paper, with the words 'yes' and 'no' added for good measure. Numbers also may be included. These are then arranged in a circle on a table top. A glass with a stem is placed in the centre, base uppermost, and all participants place the tip of their forefinger lightly upon the bottom of the glass. After a while the glass begins to move and to spell out messages by visiting letters. (Some spirits can't spell very well!)

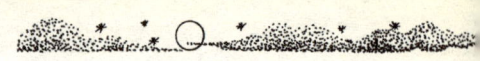

If you have never tried the 'talking glass' and doubt that it works, believe me it does. The glass is not pushed by those taking part and cannot, in my opinion, be pushed even subconsciously, for unless the table top is very highly polished and the fingers positioned just right, it is hard to move the glass at all, and when it does move it judders. I have seen the glass whizz around the table, for hours, sometimes moving with just the finger of one person on it, and sometimes moving with no one touching it at all. The terms 'ouija', 'planchette' and 'talking glass' are often used interchangeably. This is not a parlour game; this is definitely the 'paranormal'.

This chapter reveals some things about the talking glass that you may find fascinating, because it seems such an easy way to get results. You may, naturally, want to try it out for yourself, but I advise you strongly against this. I believe ouija can be dangerous, unless you are occult adept, and if you are adept you will use other, more reliable ways to receive information from the subtle planes. I have seen several people very badly frightened, including myself at one point. One young man I know was told by a ouija board game that he would be killed by the 'fire demon' at the age of fifteen. I have never seen anyone turn quite so pale! By now I have an extremely strong stomach with regard to such predictions and phenomena, but I must confess I celebrated his sixteenth birthday with extra enthusiasm!

A friend of mine saw her birthday party end in panic when the ouija board was brought out and something spelled 'death, death, death'. When I was seventeen my dead grandfather 'made contact' and told me to go to church, which I had stopped doing. Ghostly knocks sounded and my two friends refused to continue, scuttling off to sleep in a room together, leaving me alone in my bedroom where the shadows seemed to dance all night. I did not sleep well that night.

There are also reported cases of possession and other mental disturbance which seem to have arisen from tampering with the talking glass. I do not know how reliable such accounts may be, however, and people who are strongly opposed to what they term 'occult dabbling' may be too quick to condemn. Nonetheless, this uncontrolled form of contacting the subtle realms can result in the etheric, or energy body, being perforated, possibly inviting some form of spirit invasion.

The 'Ladder of Selves'

In *Mysteries* (Grafton, 1986) Colin Wilson recounts the experiences of Alan Vaughan with a ouija board. Vaughan and his friend asked the board about the death of a well-known newspaper columnist and they were informed she had died of poison. At the inquest ten days later this was revealed to be true. Another spirit called Nada got inside Vaughan's head so he could hear her repeating the same phrases over and over again. The board spelt out 'Awful consequences – possession'. Wilson records, 'In the presence of a friend who understood such matters, another spirit called "Z" made Vaughan write out the message: "Each of us has a spirit while living. Do not meddle with the spirits of the dead".' After this Vaughan, who had been pale and scared, felt a surge of enormous energy and well-being. He felt uncontained by time and space and began to sense what other people were thinking and what was going to happen in the future.

Colin Wilson relates these occurrences with his own convincing theory of a 'ladder of selves', a type of internal hierarchy, the upper echelons housing a superior being with heightened faculties that we can learn to call upon. This higher self or selves have paranormal powers that may be accessed when we achieve peak experience or certain states that we may call mystical or inspired. However, he also says:

> *Most recorded instances of telepathy and prevision have taken place without the surge of heightened consciousness ... So it would seem that if such powers depend upon our 'higher centres', then there are two ways of establishing contact: either clambering*

up the ladder, or through some form of short-circuit that connects the higher self and the everyday self without the everyday self being aware of it.

There seems much to recommend Wilson's theory. It explains why some people are natural witches or mediums and why others have to work to achieve the right state of mind. For instance, some people are able to charm away warts with a touch, while it took me three attempts, with three different rituals, before a small wart on the hand of one of my sons disappeared. However, there may be advantages to taking the long route for it comes with inbuilt safeguards such as protective rituals and achieving the right state of consciousness. In other words, the result seems dependent on self-expansion, focus, inner strength and harmony to the point where the 'spiritual essence' is enhanced and the goal, whether it involves mediumship or something else, becomes to some extent irrelevant. The talking glass needs none of these things. It is an effective form of short-circuit' and, therefore, a dubious idea.

Entities

The talking glass opens a doorway and we have no idea who or what is going to come in. Furthermore, we cannot evaluate anything that comes in. The talking glass opens a rift between dimensions. I am not sure why this happens so easily in precisely this way, but each time the rift is opened it becomes easier to open it again. The circular formation of the letters, the expectant, highly charged atmosphere and the shape of the glass are all part of the equation. Now we open this shadowy portal and invite in – strangers. Imagine opening your front door on a dark night to a group of wanderers. They may appear friendly, entertaining and talented, and they may indeed be all they seem. Conversely, they may spin you a web of lies, they may have concealed weapons or they may change, before your eyes, to a pack of ravening ghouls. Would you really let these people into your house? The talking glass may be letting in something worse. It can be like walking blindfolded into a zoo when someone has unlocked the animal cages. You might walk in on the lions, the chimps or the baby seals. Chances are, rather, that the lions will find you first. The sort of entities you may contact with the talking glass are, I believe, as explained below.

- You will probably contact some form of 'lower' spirit entity, whose intelligence is probably not great but who may be lost, confused, unhappy and out to cause trouble. I do not know where such entities originate specifically, but they are not spirits of the dead, although they may pretend to be, especially if you *want* to contact deceased relatives and friends. These spirits can be deceptive and frightening. Poltergeist phenomena may result and you may find objects go missing or even that things move of their own accord – however, these are extreme examples and should not arise from a single session of the talking glass. It is most likely that the messages will be of no real importance, being trivial, time-wasting and possibly scary.
- You may simply contact unconscious elements in one or some of the participants. These can reveal themselves as real, separate personalities, and you would not imagine that they originate inside someone's mind. However, some people do repress large chunks of themselves and these 'chunks' can acquire considerable power. Without any occult agency they can seem to operate strongly in a person's life, similar to what we may call a 'complex' where there seems to be a split-off portion that acts almost autonomously. That can be annoying in ordinary life, for instance when we are halfway down the road and our worrying 'complex' insists we go back to check we have switched off the fire, even when we know we did. In the case of people who are extremely controlled and who often take the 'moral high-ground' there may be a fairly large split-off portion, full of all sorts of irrational and forbidden emotions that may acquire considerable voltage. I do not talk here of schizophrenia or any other serious condition, for we are all composed of many different layers. The glass seems to be able to pick up on any or all of this, even simply our conscious thoughts and wishes.
- You may be really unlucky and contact what I can only describe as something from an astral pit, which is highly and explicitly malevolent, clever and feeds on fear. I do not believe this happens often, for we all have spirit guardians and also an unconscious psychic skin which serves to protect us. But the

talking glass is in a sense exposing this skin to rupture. Cases of possession and hauntings may conceivably result from this, in extreme cases. Mostly phenomena do cease once the talking glass is put away, but not always. I have no experience of such as entity and I know of no one who has experienced quite this manifestation, at least not through the talking glass. However, I do believe it is possible and, if such were contacted, it could be hard to banish the influence.

- You may truly contact the dead, but that may not be edifying. The dead are not always wise. Some are imprisoned by their own beliefs and are no more enlightened than when they were alive, so what they say is not oracular. In my opinion, you could never be totally sure that you were really in contact with a deceased loved one, except through a strong intuitive feeling, and we can all deceive ourselves when we wish deeply for something. Contact with the dead is likely to be upsetting and there are those who assert that they should be left alone to pass on to the next stage of existence, wherever and whatever that might be, not dragged back in this way to answer questions, unless they specifically wish to return.
- You may contact higher parts of yourself, what some have called 'the Overself' and so receive messages that are galvanising and enlightening.
- You may contact 'thought-forms' which are entities conjured up either on purpose or by accident from within a person's own mind. These are more defined than the phenomenon I referred to as 'split-off portions'. Such thought forms are believed to have been generated by the builders of the pyramids by visualisation and ritual to protect the place, and similar beings have been seen or sensed near neolithic mounds and stone circles. These may appear as an animal, person or something like a 'shadow'. Through the talking glass they may express themselves like any other spirit or person, quite articulately. Thought forms are more fully discussed below.
- You may contact a spirit guide (i.e. a spirit assigned to offer subtle guidance on life's path). These beings are highly evolved, but they may possibly be stern and tell you to stop doing what you are doing.

- You may contact a being from the angelic realms and a gentle presence may fill the room. The messages might be simple but hard to understand. If this happens you'll be lucky. I have not heard of it.

I am sure there are other possibilities, and among them is the fact that the glass may not move at all, which is quite likely and might be best!

This selection of contacts is drawn from my own experience and that of others of my acquaintance, plus the evidence and writings of those experienced in the occult, but it isn't the full extent of possibilities. One simply cannot be sure what is being contacted and there is no way of controlling it. Often more than one 'spirit' makes contact at a sitting.

Personal experience

I and some friends did practise the talking glass repeatedly when we were at university and, despite all I have said above, it is an experience I would not have missed for the world. I found that it opened up my outlook and awakened me more thoroughly to the existence of other dimensions. I believe I was lucky, in several respects.

At the time I was living with my boyfriend, who was a psychic individual. Since childhood I had studied various forms of the so-called occult and this interest now intensified. I researched past lives and astral projection, practised psychometry, telepathy and the viewing of auras, and meditated a great deal. Three of us, my boyfriend, myself and the student from the adjoining bedsit, started to practise the talking glass. The results were amazing.

Jeff, my boyfriend, was able to place his finger lightly upon the glass and it would move. Usually it moved better when I and Dave also put our fingers there, but sometimes this wasn't the case, and it moved best for Jeff alone. As we continued to do this, the glass moved more and more easily and, after a few days or weeks, it often moved on its own, starting to wander impatiently as we were setting up the letters! We were not scared, although I am not sure why. The attitude we maintained at all times was one of 'mirth with reverence'. We knew we were in the presence of something interesting, awesome and even powerful. We were calm and fairly sensible – bearing in mind what we were doing wasn't perhaps 'sensible' – and we kept a sense of humour and proportion. Jeff, the psychic one, had to 'feel right' about it. Sometimes we would meditate beforehand, and often we performed rituals to cleanse our space, although we did not call them 'rituals'. Nonetheless, we were aware of the necessity to be prepared and in the right frame of mind, and I think this kept us safe. At the time we often attended spiritualist meetings and were approached several times by the presiding medium (a different person each time), saying 'You've been doing the talking glass, haven't you? Well, you shouldn't'. We might as well have had it written on our foreheads!

The spirits we contacted were those of our spirit guides, and a belief in reincarnation was implicit in the messages. The two men had guides who had incarnated with them on Atlantis, the lost continent, many thousands of years ago. Apparently they were all involved in a priestly caste, but the guides were still in spirit form and seemingly more evolved. I felt left out, because it emerged I had not been on Atlantis but the more ancient continent of Lemuria, which seemed to be more primitive. The two men had female 'guides' while mine was a majestic Lemurian, tall, like a Zulu warrior. His name, which I won't divulge because it feels like something with which I was privately entrusted, had an ancient and powerful ring to it.

We had many long and highly coherent 'conversations' with the spirits, that extended far into the night. They answered questions about our psychic development and gave advice; although none of it was explicit it was certainly not harmful. The spirits had a brilliant sense of humour and the repartee was scintillating.

My guide didn't come through much, but the others confirmed that he was present. I now wish I had valued the possibilities I had, for although I cannot, of course, be sure who or what was in contact with us, I have only recently found out more about the lost continent of Lemuria, which it seems was inhabited by far wiser souls than the Atlanteans (who seem to have brought about their own destruction through forms of scientific experimentation). The Lemurians valued the 'feminine' instinctual ways, seeking to be part of the flow of creation, and they were highly psychic. The great majority of Lemurians are reported to have left their land before it sunk, because they knew what was coming and far fewer perished than in the Atlantean cataclysm. In fact, the Lemurian approach of magic and attunement is far closer to my current lifestyle. Of course, I realise that the existence of any 'lost continents' is strongly disputed and the idea is scorned in many quarters. Nonetheless, it gave me a shiver to read about Lemuria and remember my guide, whom I have not felt close to me for many years.

After a while our contact with the spirits began to get a little out of hand. One night something crashed its way loudly around the room, until Jeff shouted 'Boo' whereupon it stopped. Objects flew off the cupboards and I was afraid to leave the room at night because I heard 'things' on the stairs. Even when we went outside the phenomena seemed to follow us and ornaments fixed to the walls would mysteriously detach themselves as we sat close by. It didn't happen all the time and even when it did nothing indisputably paranormal happened. Plates didn't start to float around our heads, but there was an undeniable disturbance around us. The guides said it was caused by lower astral entities and the guides were keeping them in check. Again, other than occasionally when I was alone, it wasn't frightening; instead it all felt strongly normal. Meanwhile our talents seemed to be growing. I could see the colours in auras, something which I cannot do now, and I developed the ability to 'see' spirit messages while I was meditating. Nothing very earth-shattering, but useful. This is something I still access on occasion.

I cannot remember when or why we stopped practising the talking glass. I believe in the end we simply got bored. It wasn't going anywhere or telling us anything new. Our studies rather belatedly claimed our attention and, later on, we all joined the rat-race in our different ways. For a while I became preoccupied with material things. Some years later my relationship with Jeff ended, due possibly to the fact that he was rather more sensitive to the spirit realm than to me! I think the point is that we had no massive awakenings or shifts of consciousness. We experienced something that was essentially trivial; interesting because it is unexplained, stimulating because it kept our minds open. Yes, it was a positive experience, but perhaps we were lucky. It isn't a risk I would take now. There are better methods.

Thought forms

Thought forms may, in a sense, be a type of ghost, or perceived as such. Thought forms may also be picked up by the talking glass.

The psychologist, G. G. Jung, one-time colleague of Freud, developed his own system of Analytical psychology which is 'friendly' towards mystical experience. In *Memories, Dreams, Reflections* (Fontana, 1983) Jung describes encounters with mythological figures that arise out of his own fantasies. (N.B: To Jung 'fantasy' wasn't idle imagination but a creative and, in a sense, objective function of a healthy mind.) He says:

> ... the ... *figures of my fantasies brought home to me the crucial insight that there are things in the psyche which I do not produce, but which produce themselves and have their own life ... I understood that there is something in me which can say things that I do not know and do not intend, things which may even be directed against me.*

Here Jung is referring to the insights of his 'spirit guru' who went by the name of Philemon. Through Philemon Jung learnt of 'psychic objectivity, the reality of the psyche'. At times Philemon seemed real to Jung. Jung writes 'I went walking up and down the garden with him, and to me he was what the Indians call a guru'. Jung, despite his giant intellect and worldly success, feared that he was going mad, so real were these visitations. He was reassured, some years later, when a cultured Indian and friend of Gandhi's visited him and spoke casually of his own guru, Shankaracharya, who was a long-dead commentator on the Vedas.

Jung's Philemon and the Indian's Shankaracharya are not 'thought forms'. In trying to define them we run into the usual problems of trying to categorise the spirit world. However, we might usefully think of them as intelligent spirits in their own right. Jung regarded such manifestations as objective and separate parts of the psyche, but he also wrote much about the 'collective unconscious' – a kind of universal sea of images and archetypes and a substratum of consciousness that links us all at a profound level, similar to separate islands joined together below sea level along the ocean bed. In some ways the collective unconscious has elements in common with the 'spirit world'.

I use the example above to give a background to 'psychic objectivity' – the independent existence of contents of the mind, independent of the ego. This objectivity can show itself in a material way, with a thought form. A thought form is an entity from the mind of someone, or the minds of several people, that is given physical form, in certain ways at certain times. Thought forms can be allied to complexes – elements in the mind that have unified to take on apparent life of their own, like that annoying voice we spoke of that insists you go back to see you have switched off everything when you have left the house. In extreme forms this can amount to neurosis, of course, and needs treatment. However, a thought form can be perceived by other people. Some thought forms may arise spontaneously, but others can be created by ritual.

Mara

In *Spells and How They Work* Janet and Stewart Farrar explain how they created 'Mara', a special thought form.

The principal place in Ireland where grey seals come to have their pups is the Inishkea group of islands of Co. Mayo. In October 1981, local fishermen massacred hundreds of the pups, claiming that the seals were harming their fishing industry. This was illegal and caused an outcry. In 1982 and 1983 volunteers from the Irish Wildlife Federation camped out on the islands to prevent a repetition of the slaughter. The Farrars write, 'Our coven would have liked to join them, but this was not possible, so we helped in our own way'.

Their 'way' was to create Mara (*mara* is Gaelic for 'sea'). Janet Farrar painted a picture of Mara so that all involved knew exactly what they were visualising. After concentrated group visualisation of Mara as a distinct personality, she was given instructions: 'You will manifest visually to, and frighten, anyone who tries to harm the seals on or near Inishkea Islands. You will harm no-one unless he persists and there is no other way of stopping him'. Throughout the year following, Mara was 'recharged' and her instruction repeated at each Full Moon.

The massacre of the pups was not repeated, although there is no way of proving that Mara had anything to do with it. However, a couple who had been taking supplies to volunteers at Insihkea, in a small boat in bad weather, were waved away urgently by a woman on the shore. Further along they landed safely, to be told that if they had tried to land at the first point they would have encountered dangerous rocks, and that there could not possibly have been a human being at that location. However, news of the apparition came as no surprise, for the 'woman' had been seen by several people as she walked among the seals which did not shy away from her.

The Farrars go on to report how another occultist sent a visualisation of *Star Trek*'s Mr Spock to work on the faulty computers of *Apollo 13*. The computer started to function properly again, to everyone's surprise, and one of the astronauts reportedly saw Mr Spock and presumed he must be hallucinating due to lack of oxygen! Such a thought form is powerful, as he is already in existence, in a sense, in that he is a reality in the imagination of millions of television viewers.

The Farrars do stress the importance for the group members who generate thought forms to recall, thank and reabsorb them. Of course, you cannot 'reabsorb' an entity like Mr Spock, but thanks are still necessary as is some ritual to dissolve the link.

Philip

In creating a thought form we are, in a sense, creating a ghost. In what Colin Wilson describes as 'one of the most dazzling experiments in the history of psychical research' (*Mysteries* – see Further Reading) the members of the Toronto Society for Psychical Research set out, in the early 1970s, to do that very thing. They invented a historical person, complete with background and life story and attempted to contact him in a seance. Their 'Philip' had a dramatic history. He lived at the time of Cromwell and fell in love with a beautiful gypsy called Margo, who became his mistress. His wife, Dorothea, discovered this and denounced Margo as a witch. Margo was tried, condemned and burnt at the stake. (As a historical note, witches were not burnt at the stake in England – legally.) After this terrible event Philip killed himself by jumping from the battlements of his house, Diddington Manor. This house actually exists and pictures of it were placed around the room where the seance was held. All the elements of tragedy and strong emotion were present in the story.

After several months of trying 'meditation' seances, with no result, a different approach was adopted. The group relaxed, chatted about Philip and sang songs. Soon a rap came on the table, and using the usual technique of one rap for yes, two for no, the group verified that this was Philip. Philip caused the table to dance all over the room and up the steps on to the platform. Philip's account of his life was so detailed that the group began to wonder if they had by coincidence 'invented' a real person. Philip even corrected the group on certain matters of history. However, he called himself an 'Anglo-Catholic' which is a label that is not thought to have existed in Cromwell's time. The full story of Philip can be read in *Conjuring Up*

Philip by Iris M. Owen and Margaret Sparrow (Fitzhenry & Sparrow, Ontario, Canada, 1976). Philip is an interesting case. Perhaps he was a historical figure, to whom the group instinctively tuned in, or perhaps he is one more example of the powers of the human mind. Certainly he is a warning not to take everything at face value!

Other thought forms

In Tibet, thought forms are called *tulpas* and there exist recognised methods of creating them, along with many accounts of tulpas themselves. The occultist Dion Fortune also created a thought form wolf, who terrorised the household until she managed to reabsorb it. This is recounted by her in *Psychic Self-Defence* (published by Thorson's). In addition, there have been accounts of novelists being 'haunted' by the characters they have created, and in a small way this has happened to me when I have written fiction (unpublished, to date). I have felt that the character was with me, commenting upon my actions, to the extent that I am reluctant to write in depth about anyone malevolent. Such phenomena are not 'just imagination', and this is borne out by the above accounts.

PRACTICE

Rather than experimenting with the talking glass or embarking on ritual to make thought forms, which is outside the scope of this book, why not try a couple of simple techniques to strengthen your psychic powers? You will need a companion, or companions, to help you do them, although psychometry could be practised alone and verified later. Always choose companions with care, however, even for exercises such as this, for with anything psychic you are to some extent, more open and it is not a good idea to expose your inner self in the presence of someone who is invasive or malevolent.

PSYCHOMETRY

Psychometry is the process of picking up impressions from objects. Personal belongings absorb much of the thoughts and feelings of their owners, especially if they are in close or continual contact with the person. Someone sensitive can then pick up any emotions that have been around, and the highly skilled may describe specific events that have taken place. In one group of which I was a part, each person placed something small in an envelope which went into a pool from which the group members picked one envelope each. You knew your own envelope, but would be unlikely to recognise that of another group member. Even if you did, you would not know what was inside the envelope, for it did not have to be something belonging to that person. The object of the exercise wasn't to 'guess' what was in the envelope, but to pick up impressions. Even a small exercise like this can, however, be quite powerful. In one case I picked up impressions of mountains, lakes and fjords, plus an overwhelming feeling of sadness that was quite crushing. The contents of the envelope had belonged to a group member's mother who had felt terribly trapped in life and had longed to visit Austria and Scandinavia, which she never did.

For psychometry you need only to hold the object in your hand and see what comes to mind. The object does not have to be wrapped. It may in some respects be less distracting if you don't know what you are holding, unless you are irrepressibly curious and need to 'feel', in which case it is better to know. If an object is wrapped, or placed in a box, the packaging must be neutral and unused or impressions may be picked up from the packaging.

Some people feel that it is more effective to hold the object in the left hand, as the left hand is connected to the right side of the brain, which is the instinctual side (the reverse is the case for left-handed people). Other people like to hold the object against their forehead, between the eyes, where the 'third eye' is located. (The third eye is believed to be a centre of psychic sensitivity located between the physical eyes. This is the 'mind's eye' and has been linked to the pineal glands.) Before you do this, settle yourself comfortably, relax and take a few deep breaths. Allow a feeling of peace to flow through you.

GHOSTS - A BEGINNER'S GUIDE

Imagine that you are in the centre of a protective bubble, floating on a sea of tranquillity. Allow a dreamy state to wash over you, almost as if you are on the verge of sleep, although, paradoxically, you are sharply aware.

As you hold the object, say whatever comes into your mind – words, images, feelings, colours, sounds – even smells and tastes. Don't censor anything or regard anything as silly. If you are doing this alone you will need to record your voice. If you are interested enough to attempt this, with an open mind, the chances are that you do have some latent psychic talent already and this can help to develop it. If no sense can be made of your initial findings, do not reject them, for they may later be found to have relevance.

Telepathy

Of all the psychic skills the existence of telepathy is probably the best proven by the experiments of J. B. Rhine at Duke University, in the opening decades of the twentieth century. Some experiments with a psychic student have results of 10,000 billion to one against chance, yet this has not been fully taken on board by the scientific community.

Have you ever 'known' who it was at the other end of the line when the phone rings, or thought about a friend just before they phone? Or guessed what someone was going to say before they have opened their mouth? Do you tune in to people's moods or get gut feelings about people? If so, the chances are that you have telepathic abilities and these can be improved upon. Such skills often work best between family members. Some say they represent the next stage in the evolution of the human race. As we enter the next millennium and the open spiritual climate that has been called the New Age, such occurrences are on the increase. I recently had the strange experience of finding the address of someone I do not know well repeating itself in my mind – and then she 'phoned me, to tell me she was moving house, so would I like to have her new address?! Telepathy is easy to try out.

One simple experiment can be undertaken by two people, one the sender and one the recipient. You both need, preferably, to cultivate the relaxation and state of mind described for psychometry. Then the sender simply concentrates on an image, conjuring up a vivid mental picture of it, big, shining and flooding your being. You can imagine the image travelling towards the recipient and being absorbed by them, or just filling the room and connecting the psychic space between you. Do not become tense with the effort! Keep the image simple at first – you could perhaps stick to geometrical outlines. Colours are an excellent thing to transmit, and perhaps the easiest, but as there are relatively few colours in the visible spectrum, you may be worried about coincidence and chance; images will give you less likelihood of chance. You can draw a selection of perhaps twenty line drawings on separate cards and pick from them. Suggestions are sun, moon, star, square, triangle, cross stick person, heart, tree, flower, key, bird, fish, chalice, arrow, candle, eye, snake, boat and wave formation. Later on, as you become more proficient, you may like to try more complex images, such as the major arcana from the Tarot pack. Such images are archetypal – in other words they are basic to the human psyche, have universal meaning and are powerful, so making them easier to embody. You may also like to try telepathy with feelings, scents and sounds. Some people find they have a talent with one sense, while achieving hardly any results with the others. Keep a note of your findings – they could be interesting, and useful!

3 ATTITUDES TO DEATH

... If you would indeed behold the spirit of death, open your heart wide unto the body of life.

For life and death are one, even as the river and the sea are one.

In the depth of your hopes and desires lies your silent knowledge of the beyond;

And like seeds dreaming beneath the snow your heart dreams of spring. Trust the dreams, for in them is hidden the gate to eternity.

... And when the earth shall claim your limbs, then shall you truly dance.

Kahlil Gibran, *The Prophet*

If you are interested in ghosts you probably also find yourself thinking about life after death, in some form. What is it like to die, and what happens afterwards? Life is uncertain in all but one aspect – one day we shall die. However, this fact is almost totally ignored in Western culture. Those who ask questions about death – usually children – are mostly fobbed off with platitudes. More persistent investigators are regarded as morbid. One of the craziest things about our culture is that we do not address this inevitability. Possibly we are keeping from ourselves sources of hope and knowledge. We may have nothing to fear.

Native attitudes to death

Small children below the age of five have no notion of death as an ending, but only as a temporary separation, wanting to know how and where life continues. My three-year-old son, repeatedly watching a favourite video during which a cat is swept over a waterfall, insists that the cat 'dies' and mourns in due measure with each viewing, even though he knows quite well that the cat is, in fact, saved from drowning, to reappear later in the film, when he will say 'There she is'. To him there is presumably no difference between what we would term 'real' death and this temporary departure. This type of attitude is evident in many native practices.

Most native cultures have explicit beliefs surrounding death and the spirits of the dead. In the Native American sweat lodge ritual, the Great Spirit inhabits the pit containing the hot stones, where also resides the spirit of a beloved relative, now dead. Ancestral spirits achieve a god-like status to many indigenous peoples, although they may also be feared. Shamanic techniques, that is the ability to perform spirit flight in leaving the body while still alive to travel the spirits realms for knowledge, are basic to most so-called 'primitive' cultures. Here belief in life after death is implicit and the ancestors may be specifically consulted regarding problems that beset the living.

The Central Melanesians believe that humans are composed of a body and a soul, and that death marks the final separation of the soul from the body, although it continues to exist, separately and consciously. These people imagine the soul looking on and laughing at mourners who are bewailing its death. New Guinea natives believe that the dead often appear to the living in dreams, to give them advice on matters as diverse as gardening and witchcraft. Among the Shilluks of the White Nile, a man who wants advice from his dead parents will dig up their skulls and sleep with them beside him, so they may contact him in his dreams. Further examples such as this can be drawn upon, worldwide.

To the Australian Aboriginals, death is not an ending, but a transcendence, enabling the spirit to gain re-entrance to the ancestral reservoir of the Dreaming. As death draws close, the old person discusses death and makes provision for it. Aborigines often say that Europeans have no prior knowledge of death and so cannot prepare for it. In contrast Aborigines are able to communicate with the Sky Heroes, often obtaining a knowledge of the time and place of death. Two souls, or two aspects of the soul, separate at death. These are known to the Yolngu of north-east Arnhemland as the *mokuy* and *birrimbirr* spirits, corresponding to the *ka* and *ba* souls of the Egyptians. The mokuy spirit returns to the specified clan territory and can be mischievous and even malevolent. The birrimbirr, on the other hand, becomes incorporated with the Sky Heroes, the Dreamtime and the ancestral land.

This belief seems to echo accounts of psychics regarding different spirits, some of which are earth-bound and troublesome, while others bring with them light and peace. The mokuy seems to have more in common with the etheric body, referred to in Chapter 1, while the birrimbirr is the astral body, in tune with the higher self. Aboriginal death rituals are complex, involving song, dance, the making of sand sculptures and the painting of the coffin. These are all designed to aid the spirit on its path to the Dreaming and to drive away the mokuy spirit. However, the memory of the deceased is not diminished. For example, the Gidjingali of Arnhemland preserve the bones – which are associated with the birrimbirr – in a hollow pole called a *dupun*, which becomes a permanent icon. James Cowan, in *The Aborigine Tradition* (Element, 1992), writes:

In all cases we are confronted with a finely tuned relationship between the living and the dead, between totemic existence and the bones of the deceased, and between the clan territory and the spirit of the deceased ...

The bond between the living and the dead among Aborigines suggests an unfamiliar spiritual perspective to many who might regard death as something abhorrent. Yet it is clear these people have drawn their knowledge of it from an ancient source – a source perhaps inspired by real contact with the otherworld in the distant past ...

In the end, the role of death among Aborigines is one of healing ... making it possible for Aborigines themselves to join with the Sky Heroes ... in serving notice that the universe is indeed one rich and undivided whole.

Tibetan Beliefs

The Tibetan *Book of the Dead*, or *Bardo Thodol*, is perhaps the most comprehensive instruction and information manual on the process of dying. Bardo Thodol means 'Liberation by Hearing on the After-Death Plane'. It was first set down in writing in the eighth century CE, although it doubtless represents the wisdom of countless generations, who lived by an oral tradition and believed utterly in existence after death. It is read out to guide the recently deceased during various stages of existence after death, and contains detailed descriptions of the experience of death itself, pointing the way to liberation of the soul, or to rebirth, whichever is suitable. No one can be sure how this knowledge was come by. Unless someone sat down and made it all up, the experience must presumably have been transmitted by highly evolved spirits of deceased lamas to their 'psychic' followers, or have been remembered from previous incarnations.

Buddhist philosophy states that we are trapped in this world of illusion by the power of our desires, and only by letting go of these can we attain our spiritual homeland. The *Bardo Thodol* expresses hope that the individual has no lingering karma, or spiritual dues that remain unpaid and can move towards transcendence, but if not then another incarnation upon earth must ensue. The *Bardo Thodol* assumes, in accordance with Buddhist belief, that in the end there is no separate consciousness, as such, but only the blissful state of Nirvana, or union with the Divine. For us in the West, this may be rather advanced, and we may prefer the evidence of innumerable psychics that our personality and those of our loved ones do indeed survive bodily death. This is not apparently contradicted by the *Bardo Thodol*, but regarded as undesirable in comparison to being absorbed in the Divine.

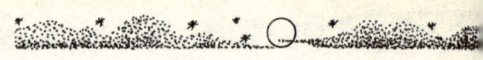

Three stages in death are described, involving the four traditional elements. The first is a sensation of bodily pressure as 'earth sinks into water'. The second is a feeling of coldness and clammyness which gradually changes to feverish heat, as 'water sinks into fire'. The third stage, of 'fire sinking into air' involves the feeling that the body is being blown to atoms. Meanwhile the body undergoes visible changes, as control is lost of the facial muscles, hearing and sight fail and the breath comes in gasps. The *Bardo* stresses the desirability of remaining conscious in the body, concentrating upon love and compassion, and upon what is called the Clear Light, which then appears. As the 'Bardo body' separates from its earthly 'clothing' it should ideally pass out of the 'brahmanic aperture' at the crown of the head, accompanied by no break in consciousness.

Once separated, the Bardo body is formed of an ethereal type of matter, that can pass through solid forms and arrive anywhere in an instant, but retains all the consciousness, memories, etc. of the deceased. Naturally the person is at first bewildered and can see its old, physical body being looked after by the bereaved. There may be sadness at viewing sorrow yet being unable to help grieving loved ones. From there, a process of getting used to one's new state must follow. Death is viewed as the reverse of the birth process. However, to have knowing companions and a map of the territory of dying must be of immeasurable comfort. This reminds me of what a friend of mine told me about the death of her mother: the dying woman demanded irascibly of her relatives 'Show me how to die, then'.

MODERN BELIEFS

Many people are rather vague on the subject of death, possibly because they have chosen not to reflect too much upon it. Some insist that their whole essence is material and that death is a total ending of consciousness. Eternal annihilation is hard to imagine but presumably it is logically quite possible. However, it is hard to believe that in their heart of hearts even the staunchest atheists carry no hope of a hereafter.

Catholic doctrine specifies the existence of Heaven, Hell, Purgatory and Limbo. Heaven is where people who have led perfect lives go when they die, being a place of bliss where God is endlessly praised. Purgatory is for souls who have sinned, but are not irretrievably damned. The length of their stay in this place of suffering depends on how bad they have been and how long it takes to purge them. Babies who have not been baptised go to Limbo, while those who died in wickedness go to eternal damnation in Hell. Other Christian beliefs may be more gentle and less categorical. Indeed many people who would call themselves Christian do not believe in Hell, or anything similar and merely believe that union with God follows death, in accordance with the teachings of Jesus Christ.

Modern **pagan beliefs** span a wide variety of alternatives, but rarely embrace total and utter annihilation at death. Paganism is probably the fastest growing religion, currently, and can be defined loosely as Nature worship. There is much less emphasis upon exactly what one believes and much more upon experience and behaviour, which arises not from an imposed doctrine but from a vivid feeling of kinship with the earth. Some pagans feel that we return to the earth at death and as our bones dissolve in the soil, so our spirit passes into the wind. We do not end, but become part of the ever renewing cycle of nature, our lives being as the leaves on the trees, which fall in winter to fertilise the blooms of the coming spring. This is peaceful, but seems to deny the survival of anything associated with individuality. Most pagans, as far as I can ascertain, believe rather in reincarnation – a succession of lives travelling, in a sense, a cycle, much like the seasonal cycle, during which progression is achieved in something resembling a spiral. Such 'New Age' beliefs have been termed 'woolly' but perhaps that view arises from a perspective that needs to have chapter and verse neatly arranged. True Paganism is about walking in beauty, and in your own truth. Identifying with nature, caring for the earth and your fellows is deemed more important than establishing exactly what happens when you die, which many reasonably assert cannot be finally proven and may vary from person to person.

The doctrine of reincarnation might seem to negate the existence of ghosts, for how can someone haunt scenes of their earthly life and still incarnate in another body? One answer may be that they do not, but that those souls who are earth-bound, for whatever reason, need to be freed from their bondage before they can live again. Another rather more difficult belief concerns the existence of an Overself – a higher self that is learning and progressing through sending emissaries, which are essentially pieces of itself, into the dense world of matter, like a civilised country sending explorers into the jungle. In this case there may be several incarnations on the go at once, and this theory could explain certain dreams or experiences where we may seem to be in contact with another personality, find we can understand words from an unknown language, or similar (simple reincarnation also provides an explanation). It could also explain certain types of schizophrenia. Whatever the case, reincarnation is no barrier to belief in the continued presence of spirits of the dead. The world beyond death must exist outside the frames of time and space as we know it, and there seems no reason why several alternatives should not be open.

Out-of-body experience

In Chapter 1 we discussed phantoms of the living, where an apparition of a living person is seen in a location apart from their physical body. The technique of spirit flight, or shamanism, is the oldest spiritual discipline known to humans, and the belief in the ability of the spirit to journey far beyond the body was basic to all ancient peoples. This is a technique currently being rediscovered and developed (see *Shamanism – a beginner's guide* in this series). Shamanism is a conscious, deliberate and purposeful practice. However, there is a multitude of well-documented cases of people who have apparently travelled outside their bodies. Sometimes they are seen by others, sometimes their experience is verifiable only by the fact that they are familiar with events or scenarios at which they could not have been physically present.

An example of the former happened to the poet and occultist, W.B. Yeats, as recounted by Colin Wilson in *The Occult*. Yeats told how one afternoon he was thinking intently of a fellow student for whom he had a message, which, for some reason, he was hesitant about writing. Two days later he received a letter from some hundreds of miles away, where this person was. While Yeats had been thinking so intently he had, in fact, appeared in front of a crowd of people in a hotel, seeming as solid as the flesh. The student in question asked him to come back when the others had gone, whereupon Yeats vanished, but had returned in the middle of the night to deliver the message. Yeats himself had no recollection of either incident.

Colin Wilson also recounts that the writer John Cowper Powys had similar faculties. Powys left the home of his friend Theodore Dreiser in a hurry, following a deep conversation. 'I'll appear before you, right here, later this evening,' Powys promised. His friend did not for one moment take him seriously, but, two hours later, having settled down to read, he looked up to see Powys standing in the doorway. Dreiser got up at once, remarking that Powys had kept his word, and asked him how he did it. No reply came, and the apparition vanished when Dreiser was about a metre distant from it. Dreiser immediately phoned Powys at his house in the country and it was undoubtedly his friend who answered the phone. However, Powys declined ever to discuss the incident. In Wilson's view this was because he did not know how he had done it.

Near-death experience

Allied to the above are near-death experiences, of which there is a multitude of accounts, perpetually growing in number. In many cultures a near-death experience was a necessary precursor to becoming a shaman. Certain initiatory procedures did, indeed, seem designed to induce just that, such as being rolled in the embers of a fire or having crystals pressed into the body, as in certain Aboriginal rites. The classic near-death experience goes something like this:

A person is in a state of extreme physical distress and danger, and possibly, hears a doctor pronounce him or her dead. An uncomfortably loud ringing or buzzing is heard and there is a sensation of moving swiftly down a long, dark tunnel. Suddenly, the person 'comes to' but outside the physical body, watching attempts to revive him or her. This may be disturbing at first, but in a while the new 'body' and its different characteristics and powers becomes familiar. A feeling of peace fills all and the spirits of deceased loved ones approach. A being of intense light and love also comes close and encourages a review of the life. Now, at some point, a barrier is reached that represents the boundary between this world and the next and, despite all that has happened, the person realises that although by now he or she intensely desires to go into the light and the peace, time is not yet up, and he or she must return to earth.

In other accounts subjects find themselves outside their body, but with enhanced powers, such as telepathy and instantaneous transportation. Now comes the loud noise and the passage down the tunnel. Then they emerge into a peaceful scene, met by deceased relatives. A being comes forward and the life is reviewed in an exquisite environment, or occasionally in a horrible one. As subjects walk along with relatives, a barrier is encountered beyond which they cannot go and still return. Suddenly, with a shock, subjects find themselves back in their body.

There are other variations, such as floating peacefully towards a great light, making a decision to go back to earth because of the needs of loved ones, or being told to return. Common features include separation from the body, perception of physical surroundings, the tunnel, reunion with the deceased, life review, decision to return and abrupt awakening.

In *Survival? Body, Mind and Death in the Light of Psychic Experience* (see Further Reading) David Lorimer gives many examples of near-death experience. One account by a cardiac patient tells how he felt a severe pain in his chest. He pushed the button to summon the nurse and they put up a drip, while he lay miserably, feeling as though an elephant's foot was standing in the middle of his chest. Sweating and close to vomiting, he began to lose consciousness. Everything turned black and he could hear the nurses shouting that there was an emergency. At the same time he could feel himself leaving his body, floating, and then standing watching as the nurses pushed down on his chest. Two more nurses, an orderly and a doctor arrived, but the subject could not understand why the doctor was there, because he felt fine! The doctor stepped in to help the nurse who was pushing on his chest. The doctor was wearing a blue-striped tie. The room darkened and the subject felt as if he was moving rapidly down a dark corridor. Suddenly there was a horrible shock in his chest and there was a terrific burning pain, as if someone had hit him. He woke up to find himself back in bed. All the events and numbers of people he described were later verified, as was the fact that the patient had been without heartbeat or consciousness during the entire sequence of events.

Another experience recounted by Lorimer concerns a Miss Blakeley, who became seriously ill, falling one evening into a deep sleep and awakening to find the room in darkness, calm, clear and no longer in pain. Gradually consciousness 'became condensed in the head ... then it seemed that "I" had become condensed into one tiny speck of consciousness ... Then I became aware that I was beginning to travel further upwards. There came a momentary blackout and then "I" was free; I had left my body ... And I knew this – this is what the world calls the state of death ...' Subsequently Miss Blakeley experienced panoramic review, judgement and a meeting with a being of light, before returning to the body.

People who undergo NDE usually experience profound changes in their attitude to life and death. The overwhelming majority were less afraid of death and their belief in an afterlife increased. Most stressed the importance of love and of seeking knowledge. Here are some comments, again taken from Lorimer:

This experience convinced me of a future life

To me there is nothing truer than 'There is no death'

The experience was very pleasant. If that is how one feels after death, I have no fear of dying

... there's more to me that I don't even know about. And then I started thinking about 'What is the limit of the human and of the mind?' It just opened up to me a whole new world

I always thought about social status and wealth symbols as the most important things in life ... Now I know that none of these are important. Only the love you show others will endure ...

Of course, other reductionist explanations have emerged regarding NDEs. The researcher Susan Blackmore states that such phenomena result from the brain's deprivation of oxygen. However, this does not account for those episodes where the subject sees and recalls verifiable events and circumstances that they could not have witnessed by ordinary means. Nor does it cover all situations where oxygen is *not* deficient at the time of death. Others concern such ideas as 'wish fulfilment'. Sometimes it seems that people will go to any lengths rather than face the obvious and to accept what millions of people have always believed, and what mystics, occultists, psychics, evolved souls and survivors of NDEs attest to – there is life after death.

Hallowe'en

The roots of the festival of Hallowe'en lie in Celtic culture, where the dead were honoured and even consulted. Often a tree was planted upon a burial ground and when wisdom was needed, seekers could touch the tree and absorb the peace and the knowledge of former generations. Hallowe'en means 'All Hallow's Eve', that is the day before the feast of All Saints. In common with many festivals, new Christian practices were grafted on to the more ancient pagan practices. The Celtic name for Hallowe'en is Samhain (pronounced

ATTITUDES TO DEATH

'saween' or 'sawain'), which means summer's end. However, it was also the Celtic New Year similar to the way the Celtic day began at nightfall. To the Celts, darkness was a fertile time, and while, in one sense, life was coming to an end, in another the way was being opened, in time for new life to emerge. The end of earthly life marked the beginning of the life of the spirit. In the compost formed from dead leaves, new shoots are seen to thrive. In a deeper sense that we cannot, perhaps, fully understand, the Celts were able to honour and give place to things that we push aside as too fearful.

Some historians believe that the earliest, nature and goddess worshipping peoples, lived in close harmony with the earth and felt little of the fear and alienation that came later. However, certainly at some times in history, the need to make sacrifices and to appease malevolent forces was felt, and Samhain was a time for human sacrifice. Often the sacrifice would be that of the old king, who gave his life in honour of the land to make way for a successor. The vestiges of this remain with the celebration, on 5 November in the UK, of the death of Guy Fawkes, who was not a king himself, but tried to kill the king – an ironic twist.

Even without human sacrifice, Samhain was a sad time, when hard choices had to be made and endings faced. Cattle that would not survive the winter had to be slaughtered and food had to be stored against the cold and bad weather. Old people and sickly children would be unlikely to see the following spring.

Samhain was a time of ancestor worship. It was the start of the story-telling season and an occasion to recall the beloved dead. Today, Samhain/Hallowe'en has an important function in several respects. We can use it as an opportunity for a party, and it is a good idea to revive the tradition of telling stories. However, more subtly, Hallowe'en gives place in our lives to concepts we may push away – but these things have to be faced. None of us are perfect beings. Life is a scary business and there are things that cannot be explained. Observing Hallowe'en by trick or treat, pumpkins made into eerie lanterns, witches hats and fake blood can be ways to come to terms with this aspect of life and ourselves. Rather than being scared by this, children often find it reassuring to have some place in their lives to enact all of this harmlessly.

The Autumn Equinox, around 21 September in the Northern Hemisphere, 21 March in the Southern, is considered to be a time when the veil between this world and the next is thin and more hauntings occur. Hallowe'en may be seen as the climax of this ethereal time. Spirits wander abroad and witches are said to fly at Hallowe'en. Hallowe'en is, in fact, the principal festival for witches, who are actually nature and Goddess worshippers (nothing to do with evil or Satanism), who seek to draw close to their ancestral roots at this time. At Hallowe'en the atmosphere is usually highly charged: real witches celebrate and the time is ripe for ghosts.

PRACTICE

If you would like to find out more about witchcraft, Hallowe'en and other similar festivals, see *Witchcraft – a beginner's guide* and *Paganism – a beginner's guide* in this series. *Wheel of the Year – Myth and Magic Through the Seasons* by Teresa Moorey and Jane Brideson, published by Hodder & Stoughton, examines all eight of the old festivals in detail, giving their modern significance and many practical ways to observe them.

At Samhain it is customary to ask the beloved dead to be present. The word, of course, is 'ask' never 'summon'. If you have lost a loved one this is a good time to place a lighted candle in front of a picture or perhaps a personal belonging and call the loved one to mind, in a spirit of love.

On the investigative note suggested for ghosthunting, in Chapter 1, you may like to research near-death experiences. In addition many people have had out-of-body experiences without being close to death; often they say nothing because they don't expect to be taken seriously. An atmosphere of gentle interest and openness may draw them out.

4 SCIENTIFIC PROOF OF SURVIVAL AFTER DEATH

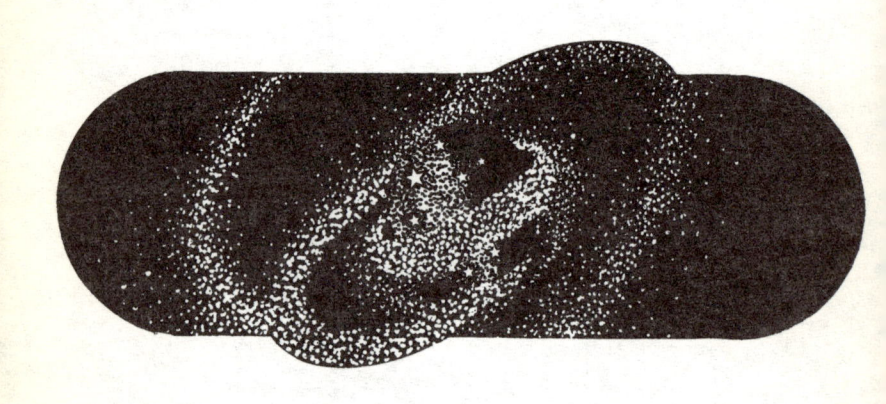

This picture of the scientist as a detached investigator, pursuing truth with a humble and pure heart, is too good to be true

Colin Wilson

If your theories and mathematics do not match the experiment, then they are wrong

Prof Richard Feynman, Nobel Laureate for physics

Everyone has the right to freedom of opinion and expression: this right includes freedom to hold opinions without interference, and to seek, receive and impart information and ideas through any media, and regardless of frontiers.

UN Universal Declaration of Human Rights, Article 19

SCIENTIFIC PROOF OF SURVIVAL AFTER DEATH

Ghosts are generally regarded as something you 'believe in' or not, as the case may be. Whether or not we are believers depends largely on our temperament and experiences. There is no way to prove that the soul survives death, because this world and the 'next' are unconnected – death is the great divide and, once crossed, cannot be retravelled. Or can it?

Even those of us who do believe that death is a transition, not an ending and who have some consciousness, however veiled, of other worlds and states of existence, usually assume this to be a subjective experience, not verifiable in any way that could be called objective, or scientific. Some researchers say otherwise. Furthermore it seems such assertions are supported by some of the finest minds in history, many of whom have been discredited by their peers, since they died, for the exact purpose of suppressing their knowledge. The point can be made that many powerful people have a great deal to lose by proof of survival. This includes the religious and scientific establishment. Certain eminent people have held such views including Winston Churchill, Abraham Lincoln and Sir William Crookes, to name but a few. Let us look at some background.

Mediumship

A medium is literally someone who acts as a 'medium' through which messages are passed from unseen realms. 'Clairsentience' is the easiest form, where emotions and feelings of the deceased are sensed by the medium. 'Clairaudience' is where a message is heard, either in the medium's mind, or apparently as an external voice. 'Clairvoyance' is mental pictures, where the medium sees the spirit, or what they are shown, such as scenes from the life. Some mediums go into a trance and the spirit communicates directly, using the medium's voice – usually the medium in question will have no recollection of anything that has been said. The modern practice of channelling is a type of mediumship, where inspirational messages are passed through the channeller.

The rarest, most difficult and potentially the most dangerous form of mediumship is that of materialisation. A physical medium of this sort is able to exude a luminous substance called ectoplasm. The ectoplasm takes shape as the bodies of those who have died, who, in the most effective cases, are able to converse with the living and interact as if they were completely solid and physically present. A medium is just like a television set, or radio. These are devices which pick up unseen vibrations – namely radio waves – and give them form. A human medium picks up the unseen world and gives form to its inhabitants. Such people are rare, but there are many well-documented instances of materialisation mediumship. Seances, where physical and other types of mediumship take place, have been the subject of many dramas and send-ups, to the point where few people take them seriously. In neglecting to do so a large body of evidence is being bypassed.

The case of Helen Duncan

Helen Duncan was a highly talented materialisation medium who was born in 1898 in Scotland. Mother to six children, and twenty stone in weight, she gave seances throughout Britain in the 1930s and 1940s. The climax of these occurred when the ectoplasm issued from her mouth and took on the form of deceased persons. Helen had brushes with the law and was convicted of fraud in 1933, when it was alleged that the apparition of a dead child was, in fact, a woman's vest that she was manipulating. However, she continued her practice. Business boomed for Helen as those whose loved ones were dead or missing in the Second World War flocked to her for contact. However, the British intelligence service MI5 had its eye on Helen.

During a seance in Portsmouth, in 1941, a sailor materialised with *HMS Barham* on his hatband. He came up to his mother and told her that he wouldn't be coming home because his ship had sunk, and he was 'dead'. His mother demanded to know why the Admiralty had not told her. It transpired that the battleship *HMS Barham* had, indeed, been sunk off Malta, but this fact had been concealed by the Admiralty in the interests of morale. The German navy believed they had sunk a cruiser and that all three British battleships stationed in the Mediterranean, *HMS Barham*, *HMS Queen Elizabeth* and *HMS*

Valiant, remained intact. Despite requests from friends and families no announcement was made for a further three months. However, Helen Duncan was 'marked' and her activities were monitored for the next two years until D-Day approached. Naturally it was essential that the landing sites and other details were treated with the utmost secrecy, and the authorities were afraid that Helen would 'see' or in some other way reveal matters of national security. Helen was taken into custody and tried under the Witchcraft Act. At her seven-day trial more than forty witnesses spoke for Helen, but the Crown insisted she was a 'humbug' and a 'pest to society'. Helen was sentenced to serve nine months in Holloway Prison in London. As she was led away she said 'Why should I suffer like this? I have never heard so many lies in my life.'

In 1944, Sir Winston Churchill, himself interested in spiritualism, took up Helen's case. He was so angered by the trial that he asked the Home Secretary for a report, demanding to know why the 1735 Witchcraft Act had been used in a modern court of justice and wondering what had been the cost to the state in this trial where the Recorder had been kept busy with 'obsolete tomfoolery'. Helen's case led to the repeal of the Witchcraft Act in England, in 1951.

After the Second World War, Helen continued to practise, but it seems certain people in authority were still uneasy about her work. Helen was an overweight diabetic with a history of heart trouble. Acting as a materialisation medium is strenuous. In November 1956 there was another police raid on one of Helen's seances, in West Bridgford, Nottinghamshire. Helen was shocked out of her trance and, as a result, died five weeks later. Campaigners assert that this was a deliberate act, upon a vulnerable woman known to be in poor health. On 31 January 1998, one hundred years after her birth, the Saturday *Telegraph* printed an article stating that Jack Straw, the Home Secretary, was considering a petition on behalf of Helen Duncan pressing for the Royal Prerogative of Mercy to be exercised in her case. If this is granted it will be for only the second time in the twentieth century (the first was for Timothy Evans, pardoned in 1996 for wrongful execution over ten years earlier).

However, Helen's story does not end there. Almost three decades after her death, Helen herself began to communicate through medium Rita Gould. Helen gave lots of facts about her life, but most of these could be gleaned from books and records. To check more obscure data it was necessary to involve Helen's daughter, Gena. When Gena was present at a seance, certain 'apports' landed on the table. Apports are objects that materialise spontaneously during a seance, literally out of thin air. There were several deep red carnations and a single red rose, which had been placed in front of Gena. Gena broke down and told how she had placed a single red rose in her mother's coffin, without telling other members of the family. Years later a medium had told her that one day the rose would be returned, and now it was. Later in the seance Helen spoke through the medium to her daughter for over an hour, using material of a highly personal nature that left Gena in no doubt that this really was her mother. You can read about Helen's story in *The Story of Helen Duncan: Materialisation Medium* by Alan E. Crossley (Arthur H. Stockwell Ltd, Devon, 1975) and make up your own mind.

Dead soldier guides a truck

During the Second World War a squad of British engineers had just finished laying a minefield in the North African desert when their young commanding officer was hit and killed by German shell fire. A few minutes later the soldiers watched in amazement as a British army truck wound its way carefully through the newly laid mines to arrive safely on home ground. The engineers demanded to know how the driver had managed to find his way so unerringly through the thick minefield. 'It was easy,' the driver replied. 'Your officer was walking in front of my lorry, showing me the safe path through.' When they asked which officer, the driver pointed to the dead man, lying only a few yards away. He had been killed before the truck began its dangerous journey.

This incident was reported in the United Kingdom in the BBC television programme called *Mysteries with Carol Vorderman*. An engineering officer who saw the incident gave his evidence, to be faced with comments from a psychological expert who voiced the opinion that all the soldiers were hallucinating under the stress of battle. The soldier, who was articulate and sensible, had a much more simple explanation – that it was the death-surviving body of the officer, the etheric body, that led the truck driver and that the driver most probably possessed mediumistic or psychic powers. This programme and the correspondence generated has encouraged the researcher Michael Roll (see Practice session below) to take his case to the European Court of Human Rights. His case is that discoveries in physics that should be available to everyone are being censored in the media, and that the full body of evidence and theoretical back-up is being prevented from receiving a suitable airing. These discoveries give substance to the fact that the human personality survives physical death by continuing to exist in the etheric, or energy body.

IDEAS AND OPINIONS

Stories such as the above are legion. We may believe them, or most of them, we may have an open mind, or we may dismiss them as the product of wishful thinking, delusion or fraud. It is hard to consider the matter coolly. I do not remember seeing or hearing a serious, in-depth examination of such paranormal phenomena that was broadcast without lengthy exposition of the views of experts intent on reducing the whole matter to illusion, or worse. One could say that was a 'balanced view'. However, when a programme on natural history, for instance, is produced, no one comes along to demolish the entire subject, in the interest of 'balance'. Psychologists often seem to regard the whole subject of the paranormal as dangerous (except for some Jungians and humanists). Everything can be reduced to wish fulfilment, the avoidance of the experience of loss, the unwillingness to negotiate bereavement and 'grief tasks'. Belief in, and experience of, the supernatural means weak ego-boundaries. Michael Roll's stance, and that of others, is that we are not being presented with the facts as they are.

In his biography of the poet and occultist W. B. Yeats, G. K. Chesterton recounts how he countered critics with his 'concrete mysticism': "'Imagination!' he would say with withering contempt; "There wasn't much imagination when Farmer Hogan was dragged out of bed and thrashed like a sack of potatoes – that they did, they had 'um out and thumped 'um; and that's not the sort of thing a man wants to imagine".' He goes on to retell how Yeats put forward the sound argument that '... it is not abnormal men like artists, but normal men like peasants, who have borne witness a thousand times to such things; it is the farmers who see the fairies. It is the agricultural labourer who calls a spade a spade, who also calls a spirit a spirit ...' Yeats' view of matters supernatural was clear, but then Yeats was a poet, a man of imagination.

In his extensive investigation into the paranormal, called *Mysteries* Colin Wilson devotes an entire chapter to what he calls 'The Curious History of Human Stupidity'. Here he examines the theory of A. E. van Vogt concerning the 'Right Man'. The 'Right Man' is a psychological phenomenon, or one could say condition, in which a person is obsessed with being right. While the Right Man may pursue truth and justice in many areas of his life, he has a total blind spot where he, himself, is concerned. Any opposition can drive him into a rage, where he may act with extreme unreason and illogic, while quite failing to see what he is doing. It seems the comfort and even the mental stability of Right Men depend on their never being proved wrong. Such a man is not, by any means, a habitual liar. His strong desire for truth may make him an excellent scientist and thinker. Wilson says 'It is only where HE is concerned that his perception of truth is distorted; besides which, the pursuit of abstract knowledge provides a welcome relief from his obsession with himself'. He goes on to point out that there are more Right Men around than we are aware of, and that indeed most of us have pockets of 'Rightness' in our personality.

The history of scientific advancement is not without its 'Right Men'. Again, I turn to an example given by Wilson. The educational psychologist Sir Cyril Burt, who died in 1971 at the age of eighty-eight, was one of the most respected men in his field, until it was discovered that he had not only falsified statistics but had also possibly invented two collaborating colleagues. 'Rightness' only increases with age and prestige – Sir Cyril Burt presumably did not feel he was misleading anyone as to the truth. He 'knew' that he must be right and so took a short cut with the details. There are countless cases of scientists battling with one another in a way that is totally inconsistent with humility in the face of truth. It has to be said that many great men of science have a substantial emotional drive, one might even say 'need' to be right. While there truly exists an enormous body of evidence that does not comply with scientific 'facts', very little serious effort has been made to investigate them. Could this be because too much rests upon the maintenance of the status quo?

Many people are quite determined not to believe in the paranormal, to the point where they unconsciously filter out their paranormal abilities. An experiment conducted by Dr Gertrude Schmeidler at Radcliffe College in 1942 (called the 'sheep and goats experiment') was designed to test ESP. Before the experiment the participants were asked to say whether or not they believed in ESP; those who said yes were classified as 'sheep', those who said 'no' were 'goats'. The experiment proved that the 'sheep' scored significantly above chance in the experiments, but what was even more fascinating was that the 'goats' scored *significantly below chance*. In fact, the 'goats' were subconsciously cheating, ignoring their 'hunches' because of their determination not to believe in ESP.

Historical case studies

Abraham Lincoln's mother was a medium and the great president was familiar with psychic phenomena. In 1862 a Colonel S. P. Kase was in Philadelphia and 'by chance' met up with a celebrated medium, J. B. Conkling. Colonel Kase set up a meeting between president and psychic due to the happenstance of Lincoln mixing him up with S. P. Chase, the Secretary of the Treasury. Mr Conkling was a guest at the presidential mansion for four succeeding Sundays when the subject of the Emancipation Proclamation was spelled out, letter by letter, by people from the 'unseen universe'. Colonel Kase also met the President and his lady at the home of another medium, Nettie Maynard, who discoursed for an hour and a half on the emancipation of the slaves while in trance. Her language was sublime and her arguments grand. When she 'came to' she ran off in confusion and fright when she realised she had been speaking to the President. The Emancipation Proclamation was issued on 22 September 1862.

The British pioneers of radio and television, Sir Oliver Lodge and Sir William Crookes seem to have been discredited because they carried out repeatable tests proving post-mortem survival. It has only recently come to light that Sir Oliver Lodge was the first person to send a radio message, not Marconi. The *Dorling Kindersley Science Encyclopaedia* has now set the record straight following the publication of the truth in the *New Scientist*, in 1995. Michael Roll feels this fact has been played down solely because Sir Oliver had the courage to link survival after death with subatomic physics, in *Ether and Reality* published in 1975 by Hodder & Stoughton. Crookes' credentials and qualifications fill one-third of a page. He was discredited in 1919 by Walter Mann who stated Crookes had sexual relations with the medium with whom he worked. That same year Crookes died. Michael Roll is of the opinion that, had Crookes survived, Mann would have been on the receiving end of a libel action.

Queen Elizabeth II has admitted in front of millions of television viewers that the diaries of Queen Victoria had been destroyed and then rewritten. Queen Victoria practised spiritualism. Through the mediumship of John Brown she made contact with her 'dead' husband. After her meetings with Brown had commenced, the Queen began to recover from her extreme bereavement. So great was her appreciation that she had a statue erected to Brown's honour. Queen Victoria's diaries were rewritten, leaving out the accounts of the seances. Was this in order to preserve the reputation of the former queen? Her Majesty was, in fact, in good company, belief in mediumship being shared by some eminent persons of her day.

A Science of Survival

The case for survival after death is quite simple, as follows:

1 With the use of materialisation mediums, 'dead' people have reappeared. This fact has been demonstrated over and over again, in laboratory conditions. The experiments are verifiable and repeatable. That the 'dead' really are who they say they are has been proved beyond any shadow of reasonable doubt.

Fingerprints have been taken of the manifesting ectoplasmic bodies and, when compared with records, these have tallied with the prints made by the person in question when alive. Such evidence has been sufficient to convict and execute many a criminal in a court of law. The so-called dead have, in many cases, conversed at length with the living. It appears that death does not confer superior wisdom or total knowledge of the purpose of existence, although those who have 'passed over' will often be in the possession of more knowledge than the living. The evidence tallies with beliefs that we have more than one body, that our consciousness moves into our 'etheric body' when we die and that it is this subtle body that is seen in hauntings.

2 The scientific proof, which existed in the time of Lodge and Crookes, lacked a scientific equation to explain it. This has now changed. A Bath scientist and former lecturer in mechanical engineering at the city's university, called Ronald Pearson, has produced the theory to explain the facts.

Pearson's work has been published by the Russian Academy of Sciences and The Center for Frontier Sciences in the USA. British organisations, however, have failed even to consider his argument. Mr Pearson states that the mind is, in fact, separate from the brain, being part of the mass of seething energy called the ether (or quantum vacuum, as we encountered in Chapter 1). Pearson is an expert on wave mechanics in engineering. He was the pioneer inventor of the gas wave turbine when he was a research officer at the National Gas Turbine Establishment. As far as I am aware, no critic has been able to find a flaw in Ronald Pearson's workings, which led to the deduction that the spirit world must exist. His conclusions mark the culmination of the enquiry started (in modern times) by Sir William Crookes in the *Quarterly Journal of Science* in 1871, entitled 'Experimental Investigation of a New Force'. Engineers have to stick close to reality if their machines are to work. Remember Yeats' views about those who call a spade a spade also calling a spirit a spirit!

Ronald Pearson has recently lectured to MENSA members. A report in *Mensa Magazine* by Richard Milton, in March 1997, discusses the 'alternative science'. Milton writes that Paul Dirac, architect of quantum theory, André Sakharov, father of Soviet nuclear physics,

Louis do Broglie, discoverer of matter waves and David Bohm, professor of experimental physics at Birkbeck College, all had one thing in common besides being Nobel laureates in physics. They all, towards the end of their lives, came to the belief that quantum theory and relativity were wrong in an important respect: 'They came to embrace the heretical belief that space is not an empty vacuum but is filled with unimaginably small particles'. Most of us with an elementary knowledge of physics know that light behaves as a wave and as a stream of particles, traversing 'empty' space. If space is indeed empty, what does the wave motion take place in? A theory of the ether explains this, describing so-called empty space as filled with granular particles far smaller than electrons, through which matter moves as bubbles through a liquid. Matter then consists of 'holes' in the ether.

This theory was advanced by British physicist and engineer Osborne Reynolds in 1902 but was superseded by Einstein's Theory of Relativity. Einstein, himself, said on his seventieth birthday that there was not a single concept about which, he was convinced, the theory would stand firm and that he was not sure that he was on the right track after all. The idea of the ether, more compatible with Newton than Einstein, has resurfaced several times during the twentieth century. Milton writes, 'Most recently the mathematical basis for the equivalence of gravity and inertia was derived by Bernard Haisch and Hal Putoff in *Physical Review* in February 1994 by assuming the existence of a "zero-point field" arising from just such a sub-quantum medium ... the particles which constitute it are expected to be in a constant state of "jitter" ... The importance of this jitter is that it will give rise to a source of free energy, or "zero-point" energy which theoretically can be tapped by a suitable device'. Perhaps the only 'suitable device' available to date is a medium.

PRACTICE

What is your opinion about the scientific proof described in this chapter? Michael Roll has made it his life's work to champion the cause of free information regarding the proof of survival after death. In person he has seen many materialisations and now the mathematics is available to back up the experiments, interest is growing in the subject and he has recently been granted several hours of media time. However, he still energetically asserts that these discoveries, which are, after all, momentous, are being essentially blocked. Michael saw National Service in the Royal Navy (1956–8) and he has two sons: one holds a BA from Birmingham University; the other is a Royal Navy Pilot. I believe Michael gives these details to illustrate that he isn't an abstract dreamer, but someone who has concrete experience of life. According to Michael, his main qualification is a lifetime of reading of survival after death as a branch of subatomic physics. His pamphlet *The Scientific Proof of Survival After Death* will be sent free of charge to anyone who sends a stamped, self-addressed envelope to him at his address: 28 Westerleigh Road, Downend, Bristol BS16 6AH, UK.

If you are ordering from outside the UK, please include two international postage coupons for reply.

Michael also includes an extensive list of recommended reading for those who wish to find out more about the subject. Here are some of the works he mentions:

Richard Feynman, *QED*, Princeton University Press, 1985
Arthur Koestler, *The Roots of Coincidence*, Hutchinson, 1972
Sir Oliver Lodge, *Phantom Walls*, Hodder & Stoughton, 1929
 and *Ether and Reality*, Hodder & Stoughton, 1925
Dr R. G. Medhurst, *Crookes and the Spirit World*, Souvenir, 1972
Richard Milton, *Forbidden Science*, Fourth Estate Ltd, 1994
Prof. Charles Richet, *Thirty Years of Psychical Research*, Collins, 1923
Carl Sagan, *Cosmos*, Macdonald, 1980

In addition, the following publications of R. D. Pearson's work are available from Michael Roll (UK prices):

The Colossus (an introduction to his main book, listed below) £2.00 post paid

GHOSTS – A BEGINNER'S GUIDE

Intelligence Behind the Universe (enlightened physics explaining the paranormal) £10.00 post paid

Origin of Mind (a lecture showing our minds are immortal) £3.00 post paid

Key to Consciousness: Quantum – Gravitation (a paper showing that a primary consciousness lies at a sub-quantum level of reality) £1.50 post paid

If you live outside the UK please apply direct to Michael Roll to enquire about payment and cost of postage.

* * *

Investigate the subject as you wish, and enjoy your quest. Let us end with two quotations from Carl Sagan.

Intellectual capacity is no guarantee against being dead wrong.

The trick is to read the right books.

5

COPING WITH PHENOMENA

*From ghoulies and ghosties and long-leggety beasties
And things that go bump in the night
Good Lord, deliver us!*

Scottish prayer

Ghosts can visit us in different guises, manifesting to any of our five senses even including taste in rare instances. Whatever happens we react to the phenomena in a variety of ways. Sometimes response seems imperative, at others it hardly seems to matter.

I regularly have to be alone in a building I know to be haunted. Others who also work there have said they have sensed and seen nothing, but I feel a presence that makes me uneasy and even panicky on the rare occasions when I have been there in the dark and alone. Mostly I just feel the presence, but I have also heard footsteps and I have a strong sensation of being watched by malevolent eyes, from certain parts of the building. I began to think I had an overactive imagination, until one Christmas party when I chatted about my feelings to the cleaning lady. 'Oh yes,' she said, matter-of-factly, 'it's haunted. I'm always hearing it. Sometimes it switches the kettle on for me!' I have since learned that the building in question is on the site of an old graveyard which is reputed to be on a ley line.

(A ley line is believed to be a line of some sort of energy running along the earth's crust; all sorts of mysterious phenomena seem to be more likely in these places. You can find out more about ley lines in *Earth Mysteries – a beginner's guide* in this series.)

After that I felt better but still uneasy, until I tried to help myself to overcome my unease. I realised that I had just been staying in 'everyday consciousness', material reality, and allowing 'it' to frighten me.

I decided to adopt what I call 'magical consciousness' when around this influence. This means that I shifted to the state of mind I use for rituals, which is quite hard to describe but easy to achieve, once you know how. It is a slightly dreamy state, relaxed but highly aware, where consciousness seems stepped up several notches and one is aware of subtle reality. This has built-in protection; I have often used it within the bounds of the magic circle, created on the subtle planes by occultists, so I was sensitive inside a sort of protective bubble. In this way I confronted the entity on its own ground; I made it's ground my ground too, not trying to flee from it or allowing it to frighten me. I did not see it, but I gained a clearer picture of it. It seems to me to be a 'mean, green creature', irritable and sinister but not deeply malevolent or harmful. It resents intruders and wants to be left alone. I told it to go away and leave me alone, and that I would soon be gone so it could have its space to itself.

I can't say that I am entirely happy around this entity, by any means, but changing my consciousness in this case helped me to cope, because I no longer felt that it could sneak up on me from behind. Getting on to the same ground as 'it' put it in perspective.

The commonplace

Not all psychic phenomena are scary; some people describe their ghosts as friendly. One day, at the home of a friend, my mother became aware of someone sitting beside her. When she looked closely he wasn't there, but when she looked away, there he was again. 'Who's that?' my mother asked her friend. 'That's old George,' came the reply. 'He's often here – he's our resident ghost.' 'Oh,' said my mother, and went on with her crossword.

In *Experimental Magic* (Aquarian, 1978) J. H. Brennan recalls how a friend of his, the widow of a novelist, encountered a wood nymph. This entity, '… in the shape of a beautiful young girl with long brown legs and long blonde hair, dipped its toes in a pool beneath the trees.' Brennan questioned the lady about the encounter.

Did she, I asked, say anything to the creature?

Mrs M looked shocked. 'Good heavens no! It certainly wasn't my place to speak to such an ethereal being.' She paused, then added 'She had such a lovely aura.'

I had never seen a wood nymph and the thought of talking to someone who had met one such a short time before excited me enormously. I tried to guess what my own reactions would have been in the circumstances. 'If you didn't speak to her, what DID you do?'

Mrs M's calm eyes focused on my own and a faint expression of surprise crossed her features. 'I was rather late for tea,' she said, 'so I walked on down to the house …'

… Who, faced with a wood nymph, would worry about being late for tea? Only, one might imagine, such a civilised and genteel lady as Mrs M. But one would be wrong. Swept up in the experience of the preternatural, the varieties of human reaction seem endless.

Brennan goes on to describe how the reaction of most people to the paranormal seems eccentric. However you think you will react, with excitement, panic or whatever, when it actually does happen you may react differently. In fact, the 'paranormal' may seem quite 'normal' which in a sense, no doubt, it is. Some of my experiences have seemed quite ordinary, and the most blatantly and physically 'abnormal' such as a glass that whizzed around the table by itself and objects that flew off cupboards of their own accord, seemed strangely commonplace. At other times, where I have had a massive gut feeling about something, every cell in my body has risen up to be counted, and that has felt 'normal', obvious and imperative. At other times where I have felt 'spooked' and anxious, as if something threatening was looming and a ghostly agency was warning me of a disaster, I have simply been tired and low, in need of a laugh with friends and a good night's sleep.

So, in the case of many phenomena, our best course is to take them in our stride, but what if this is not possible?

Malevolent encounters

Philosophical debates have long centred around the question of good and evil. Feeling is growing that such polarised ideas are simply a product of our limited perspective, that the terms are relative and that, in any case, much of what has been called 'evil' isn't really so by any definition and has received that label because it was found, in some way, threatening to material security or cosy world views. However, there are some things that, it seems, have to be called evil because they feel that way and because there is no other word for them. My closest encounter of this kind came when I lived in an old manor house in Evercreech, Somerset, England. The place was undoubtedly haunted by several entities, one of which was very grim. The building was old and had dungeons – scenes no doubt of intense misery and despair. Local reports also said that prisoners had been tortured there, but I have no historical verification of this. However, nothing I experienced either there or anywhere else has come close to the following account.

Spirit of Evil

This story is taken from *Ghosthunter: Investigating the World of Ghosts and Spirits* (see Further Reading) and is given as a true account. Eddie Burks, who co-wrote the book with journalist Gillian Cribbs, is a gifted psychic who specialises in freeing trapped spirits. His work is well documented and extensive, with lots of corroborating evidence, which we do not have the space to examine. Eddie Cribbs is a retired civil engineer who takes a practical approach to his work. For some reason he has the ability to hold souls 'steady' while showing them the light. Perhaps this is because he is essentially down to earth and modest. This particular 'job' took place in a Welsh farmhouse.

First, some historical background: On an autumn night in 1848, farmhand Thomas Edwards took a shortcut back from a meeting with a girl, and went to investigate a flickering light he saw in the darkness. Coming through the surrounding trees, he found himself on the outskirts of a graveyard next to an old manor house. Low, rhythmic chanting vibrated through the misty darkness and he saw a dozen or so robed and hooded figures, gathered around a tomb, where a woman clothed in black lay motionless. As the scent of incense drifted into the November night, a man in red strode up to the woman and, invoking Satan with terrible words, he drank from a chalice as another man tore the robe from the woman's body. The dregs from the chalice were poured over her, and her face was smeared with blood and faeces. Then the man in red knelt before a nearby altar where two black candles burnt, proceeding to enunciate a travesty of the Lord's Prayer. Whereupon the 'congregation' fell upon the victim, with tooth, nail and knives. Thomas Edwards fled, the cries of the woman ringing in his ears.

The next day, nauseated by his experience to the point where he could hardly work, Thomas told his friend, James Griffiths, what he had seen. Later on he went to the alehouse to drown his terrible memories. After getting drunk he spilled out the story to anyone who would listen and was carried home in a stupor. Days later he was found on a dung heap with a ghastly wound to the skull. Twelve hours later he died.

The following spring James Griffiths, a simple boy of nineteen, was brought to trial for Edwards' murder. He pleaded 'not guilty' and stood in the dock 'with a blank expression on his face'. He said nothing in his own defence and left the matter to the judge and jury, who pronounced him guilty. On the morning of 11 April 1849, he was brought out of Brecon county gaol and marched to the scaffold, where he would neither look at nor address the crowd of 1,600 who had gathered to watch him die. The black cap was placed over his bowed head and he was hanged. He struggled for four minutes before dangling limp and lifeless. His body was buried within the gaol precincts.

Now we move up to date, to the summer of 1990, when a successful artistic couple called Bill and Liz, with their two children, moved into the manor house near which the satanic ritual had been performed, a century and a half earlier. Their first months in the manor house were 'magical'. However, they did notice the odd recurrence of the digits 666, in the rent bill, car registration, supermarket bill and lunch bill – 666 is the number of the Beast, from the book of Revelation in the Bible. After six months the atmosphere in the house changed, abruptly. It would grow suddenly dark and a 'sweet, acrid smell – like incense mixed with sulphur' filled the room. Everyone began to feel unwell and drained. Then heavy snoring was heard in the bedroom and black shadows kept appearing in the house. The family feared they were going mad.

Anglican and Catholic exorcists, dowsers and psychics came and performed rituals, but to no effect. One local exorcist told them the snoring was probably Satan himself, drawn there by books on the paranormal that the family possessed. The couple sent off their books, pictures and ornaments to be burnt and became Christians in their desperation to be free of the horror. Meanwhile their finances were suffering and the entities were apparently interfering with the electricity. A bill for £700 arrived with a threat of disconnection, should it remain unpaid. They moved out, to Liz's parents, but many of the problems followed them. Their cat ran away and their pet pig went mad and died. Bill hated going back to the house, but had to, periodically, to collect things and care for the place. On one occasion the original atmosphere of happiness seemed to have partly returned.

Then a voice said 'Sit down, Bill. How are you feeling? ... Why don't you just relax and stay here?' Then he saw a set of knives neatly arrayed and the voice was telling him 'use them, use them ....' He ran out and drove away so fast that he almost crashed the car.

Eddie Burks was called to the farmhouse. However, at an earlier time, Eddie had been approached by film producers who knew about the disturbances at the manor house in Wales. They wanted to film Eddie on location. Their initial visit to him to discuss the matter had been enough to trigger contact. Eddie was able to sense much disturbance and layers of influence. He also contacted the spirit of a young man who pleaded for his help, because he felt he was struggling in a giant spider's web. He said he had been murdered and Eddie got the impression that he had spotted a satanic group and spoken of it, and they had done away with him. Eddie was enabled to free the spirit of the young man, whose sister Annie came for him in the form he remembered her, leading him away into the light. (N.B: It is well known among psychics and mediums that the dead appear to us, or to earthbound spirits who knew them, in the way they are remembered. Thus children who have died present themselves as children to those who have loved them, even though they are no longer children in the spirit world.) Local records substantiated all that Eddie had learned from this young man's spirit, including the name of the little sister, Annie.

On arriving at the farmhouse itself, Eddie's first task was to lay a circle of light around the grounds, and another close to the house. Filming was attempted, but the cameras mysteriously failed. Then Eddie described a concentration of energies which were 'not benign'. He felt a cross manifesting over the building, radiating power and protection. Over the cross was a Christ spirit, shedding light. The words came 'There shall be no more fear and no more darkness and all will be safe within.' The atmosphere lightened instantly. Later Eddie said 'The satanic practices performed near here have left a dark stain ... They attracted the young boy who was murdered and since then there has been a build-up of evil forces which have started to work their way into your lives. In such situations it's normal for people's lives to break down completely.'

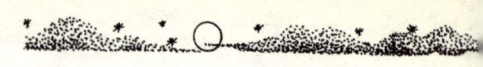

However, a day later, the atmosphere again changed and Eddie realised there was more work to do. He was now contacted by James Griffiths, who had been hanged for murder. The poor boy had been duped by the Satanists who had promised to use their magical powers to rescue him, before the trapdoor opened on the scaffold. He said nothing either about them or in his own defence. He did not know what he feared most, the Satanists, or the hanging, and he had believed they would save him right up to the moment he dropped. His grief, anger and the injustice of his death had kept him earthbound. Eddie was able to hold him steady so he could step over a threshold of light and see his parents who came to comfort and collect him. Now the task was truly complete and the atmosphere at the manor house finally clear.

I have chosen to recount the above in detail for several reasons. Few hauntings are truly evil, but some are and these need to be recognised. Any haunting is frightening and can appear evil because of this, and because it is unknown. However, where real malevolence is involved, this does become obvious and it needs to be taken seriously. The lives of people have, on occasion, been disrupted by hauntings and that can be an isolating experience, simply because other people tend not to believe them – or want to believe them. As in the case of Bill, above, people so afflicted may fear they are going mad. The more people come to accept ghosts and to take a pragmatic view of them the less this sort of utter disruption will be possible. This story indicates how like attracts like and a malevolent influence can trawl in confused and angry spirits to add to the mayhem. In addition, the fear and bewilderment of the living people involved feeds the situation.

Perhaps the most important point is that the gentle, helpful approach was the one that eventually obtained results. Eddie Burks, because of his special talent, was able to effect the release of two earthbound spirits, trapped by the tragedy and injustice of their ends and inextricably entangled in the evil that had brought about their demise – to some extent, it seems, almost in service to the beast that had devoured them. Eddie was able to act as an intermediary for the powers of love that cleansed the place. Christ consciousness is a consciousness of love and the cross has come to mean this in the hearts of many people. Specific theology does not matter. In fact, too polarised an approach can make matters worse, for it creates an atmosphere of conflict. The exorcist who induced the family to get rid of their books and become Christians did not achieve success. With Eddie there was no explicit 'driving out of demons'. Those who needed it were helped and a path was laid for light to enter.

Exorcism

In the above anecdote we saw that successive exorcisms did not work. Sometimes, however, they do, at least apparently. Rituals that have evolved through centuries of belief can be powerful because they are deeply embedded in the human psyche. However, strongly polarised viewpoints are paradoxically part and parcel of their opposite, for if someone is chosen then another is rejected; where there is light there is shadow. This is well illustrated by the picture of the Blessing Hand from the occultist Eliphas Levi's work *Transcendental Magic*. The hand held up in a blessing casts a shadow on the wall like the horned head of the Devil. Good and evil are interwoven. Does this mean we take up a stance of woolly greyness and put up with anything? I think not. Perhaps it calls for the courage to live with paradox, standing up for our right to establish what is right for us and identifying our duty to find our own truth. A recipe for confusion and conflict? But since when did dogmatism bring peace?

In *Needles of Stone Revisited* (Gothic Image, 1986) Tom Graves recounts how a friend of his, while at Southampton University, lived in a flat that appeared to be haunted. Strange noises were heard and there was an excessive sense of cold in one room, which could not be dispelled even in summer. Being a staunch Catholic, Graves' friend called in the priest to exorcise the place, which was done on condition that all members of the household agreed to be present. After this there was no more haunting, at least as far as those who dwelt in the flat were concerned. Visitors, however, still heard the strange bumps and felt the penetrating coldness. Graves makes the point, 'Rituals change the personal definition of what reality is, or should be, and thus help to make that subjective reality real in the physical world.' In the absence of having that special sense, sight and talent that enables us to see clearly into the many levels of the spirit world, rituals may be our best bet.

If you are haunted ...

If you have the misfortune to experience the sort of rare, malevolent presence that plagued the Welsh house, your situation is difficult. Weighing all the evidence and information, there seems to me no tried-and-trusted avenue to follow. Dealing with such matters requires rare talent. Many people do deal with 'the occult', including priests and Christian ministers, with variable success. If something really diabolical is about, exorcism could make it worse, acting like a declaration of war. So what is to be done? Because such instances are so rare, we could just pass them by because they make the whole subject 'heavy'. However, that seems unfair to those who experience them. So here are a few pointers.

- Firstly, are you sure something really ghastly is involved? It is 99.99% likely that it's just a bit weird and scary, and it's easy to exaggerate things when you're afraid – we all do it. What happened at the Welsh farmhouse is highly exceptional.
- If you are sure, then your best bet is to move away. The chances are that 'it' won't follow you. This is not always possible, of course, and may in any case mean that someone, at some time, has to cope with whatever it is.

COPING WITH PHENOMENA

- Reassure yourself that the balance of your mind is not disturbed.
- Remember, this is not your fault. You are not evil or guilty in any way. Indeed it is more likely that you have a psychic talent.
- If the phenomena are intrusive and your life is substantially affected, people, being what they are, may avoid you. This is isolating and makes the whole situation much more difficult. (If such things could be approached by acceptance and comradeship it is unlikely that they would gain such power in the first place. If there existed the courage to take them seriously, ways would have been found to deal with such matters effectively. It is simply easier for people to choose to disbelieve.) So continue to seek kindred spirits that will, at least, give you moral support.
- Avoid fanatics.
- Don't overestimate your ability to 'hold out'. Such things have a way of getting under anybody's skin.
- Strengthen your inner self and practise as much protection as possible. This is discussed further below.
- Pray, in whatever way seems appealing to you. Don't worry if this is rejected by your logical mind.
- Continue to look for help. Sooner or later it will come.
- Although you may feel alone and helpless, there are sure to be spirit entities working on your behalf. With our limited understanding of the subtle realms we cannot achieve a clear picture of what may be happening. Perhaps they are working to 'unblock the drains' in the astral, but some blockages are more difficult to clear than others. In our dense environment we may feel we can shut off what happens to others, but in more enlightened realms it is known that what affects one affects all, in the end. Many people, *in extremis*, have felt a vivid sense of being watched over and protected. So you are not alone.
- In the case of poltergeist phenomena, if there is an adolescent present or someone else who may be inadvertently causing the disturbance, perhaps they could be encouraged to talk about their feelings which may be turbulent. (Alternatively, the person may be utterly unconscious of having strong feelings.) All blame should be totally avoided, of course, for this isn't anyone's fault.

Strengthening yourself

Whatever so-called 'occult' activity you are involved in, from developing your psychic powers to coping with hauntings, preparation starts with yourself and begins with common sense. Here is a checklist of basics, which may seem obvious but are sometimes overlooked in the face of the glamour of the unseen.

- Avoid all drugs. Some legal drugs may be worse than some illegal ones. Alcohol, for instance, can demolish all your psychic protection and leave you open to 'etheric contamination' and too much caffeine can scramble your brain. Drink alcohol only in moderation and choose your drinking companions carefully.
- On that note, choose *all* companions carefully, especially if they are to accompany you with investigations into the paranormal. They should be well balanced, prepared to take the measures suggested here seriously and have your best interests at heart. A down-to-earth sceptic may be a preferable companion to an hysterical enthusiast! Who to take into your confidence regarding anything occult may be as important a decision as who you marry! Listen to your own 'still, small voice' and if you are in any doubt, don't let the person be close in any way, physically, emotionally, mentally, and never perform rituals or similar with them or discuss your intimate details.
- Keep your sex life well balanced. Sex should be accompanied by true affection, if not love. Avoid obsessions. Keep your self-respect.
- Get enough regular sleep if you possibly can. Individuals vary tremendously. You may need nine hours a night, or you may need three.
- Eat sensibly. Simple foods with as few chemical additives as possible are best. Many people prefer to be vegetarian. I would certainly recommend eating meat no more than twice a week. Choose organically produced meat, from animals who have been treated humanely. Organic vegetables are also preferable. Avoid faddy diets and slimming crazes – food is to nourish and be enjoyed.
- Drink plenty of fluid. Spring water, fruit juice or at least filtered tap water is best. Drink four litres a day, if you can, although many people cannot manage this.

- Take care of your body, which is the temple of your soul, by keeping it clean. Keep your house clean and well ordered. (We're talking here of sensible, manageable standards, not fanaticism!)
- Be fair and open in your dealings with others and be honest with yourself. Avoid violence of all sorts whenever you can and seek love and beauty where you can. Strong and unpleasant emotions, such as envy, are common to everyone – own yours, don't castigate yourself, don't blame others, use your energies positively, appreciate what you have, what you can do and work on it. Love yourself.
- Be aware of egotism. We all have it. Don't let yours entrap you into taking on more than you can deal with.
- Exercise regularly and have contact with nature and fresh air.

Cleansing

We all absorb a lot of rubbish from one source or another and this can build up in our system. Here I include negative emotions – our own or others, bombardment from the media and all the 101 ills of modern life. In addition, if you have come into contact with bad atmospheres or psychic influences you will need to cleanse yourself.

Start with taking a bath, containing salt or a few drops of essential oil of lavender. Imagine all the unpleasant influences draining out of you into the water. Don't imagine the influences themselves, for that can strengthen them. Just imagine greyness seeping out, dissolving and going down the drain. A lighted candle in the bathroom will help the atmosphere. This is a simple ritual bath.

Cleansing breath: After your bath, lie down somewhere warm and comfortable. Take a few deep breaths and as you exhale, imagine any greyness, tension or other contamination being expelled with your breath. Then imagine it being carried away, far into the atmosphere. Now, take a few deep breaths imagining you are inhaling particles of scintillating light from the surrounding air. You can imagine this in any way you wish, as a gentle gold, as blue or as a white shimmer. Don't breathe too deeply, for too long. Keep your breathing comfortable. If you feel strain at any time, stop what you are doing.

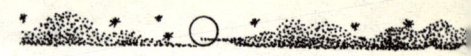

Cleansing your aura: Occultists tell us that we are all surrounded by a sheath of light, visible to some psychics, called the aura. This is our personal emanation and its general condition, size and colour can indicate our health, physical and spiritual. The innermost part of the aura is the etheric, extending for 1–2 cm (0.5–1 inch) around the body. Imagine your aura as a large egg, extending around your entire body for 1 metre (3 feet) or more. Imagine your etheric as a blue glow. Now imagine your etheric pulsing as it throws off negative energies and glows with even more vibrant power. Repeat this several times, if you wish. Visualise your etheric as a vibrant, protective barrier. Now imagine your aura pulsating, throwing off anything negative through its egg-shaped exterior, a pure golden light coming from above your head. Feel yourself surrounded by it and your aura flooded by it, expunging anything negative.

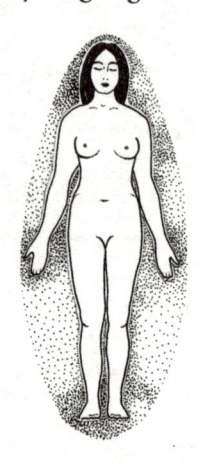

There is no space here to examine opening the chakras, which are energy centres in the subtle body. These are discussed in other books in this series, listed in Further Reading. Power can be circulated through the aura by opening the chakras. It is good practice to ground yourself after any exercise by eating and drinking a few mouthfuls and patting yourself, all the way up your body, and then placing palms flat on the floor.

Protecting yourself

Practising all of the above, regularly, will serve as a protection in itself. For added protection, adopt the habit of visualising yourself inside a strong bubble which can, in fact, be taken as the auric sheath. Visualise a tough, elastic exterior to this bubble, resilient but impenetrable. Set aside several minutes each day to visualise yourself within your protective bubble – the more often you do it the stronger it will become and it is far better to do it regularly for a short time than to strain yourself trying to keep it up for half an hour, once a week or when it takes your fancy. All occult work is based on discipline and regular habits do bring the best results, for in this way we are embedding things deeply into our unconscious.

You may also like to visualise that you possess a 'psychic cloak' which you put on when you need protection. Choose a dark colour – dark brown would be my choice. Imagine this soft, enveloping etheric cloak going all around you, the hood shrouding your head and face. If you have imagined it often enough and earnestly enough it will have true existence on the etheric plane. You can put on your 'cloak' whenever you feel you are entering a situation that feels threatening, from time spent with an unpleasant person to a ghostly encounter. Similarly, your protective bubble can come into play in such situations – just affirm that it is around you, keeping you safe. The 'bubble' is a good thing to work on generally, for it will remain with you always, to some extent, even when you are not thinking about it, if you have done your groundwork well. The 'cloak' can be kept for special occasions. Cloak and bubble can easily be used together if you are used to visualising them, but don't tie yourself in knots trying to do too much at once, if it hasn't become habitual.

A protective symbol will also be a help and you can create this symbol by 'mind stuff' so that it has existence in the astral world. You can imagine the symbol hovering above your head, in front of you, in your hand, or whatever. Choose whichever seems best and stick to it until your symbol is vivid. Later on you may like to move it around. Choose something that means love, light, strength and protection, and preferably something simple. Gold, or possibly bright blue are desirable colours. Christians may like a cross. The Celtic cross, which is an equal-armed cross within a circle is a more ancient and, some feel, more balanced icon. Others will prefer a five-point or six-point star. Of course, you may prefer the teddy bear you had as a child, but there is a lot to be said for the simple and time-honoured, for such are rooted deep within the psyche. Spend time imagining your symbol until it is a reality to you and can be called vividly to mind in an instant.

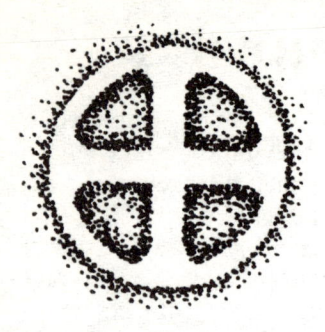

Protective herbs: To strengthen your feeling of protection you may like to carry with you certain herbs. Garlic is known to be protective. Here is a selection of other protective herbs, chosen because they are common and easy to obtain; you can carry leaves, use essential oils or whatever:

- basil
- black pepper
- cinnamon
- clove
- cypress
- eucalyptus
- lavender
- patchouli
- peppermint
- pine
- sage

You may also like to carry a protective symbol such as a holey stone. My advice is not to carry your personal, protective symbol everyday in too obvious a way, and certainly don't let anyone know what it is unless you trust them completely.

Cleansing your Living area

When you move into a new place, or even periodically wherever you live, you may like to cleanse the area. I doubt whether this will get rid of anything really 'heavy' but it can help. Certainly it will dispel any bad atmosphere, such as may be left after quarrels or if people have been unhappy or fearful in a place, and it will make the climate inclement for any minor astral entities that may have gathered.

If you are choosing a place to live, it is a good idea to find out as much as you can about what previously happened there, especially if the house is old. Like has a habit of attracting like and if people have been unhappy, if there has been ill-feeling or even violence, this can affect your life, unless you are aware or protected in some way. (N.B: most of us do have lots of unconscious protection anyway, in the shape of our etheric skin.) You may like a place superficially and may be attracted by any number of things – convenient area, low rent/mortgage, nice garden, etc. But how do you 'feel' deep down inside? Is this really a place where you want to make your home? Never commit yourself immediately. Always detach yourself and preferably sleep on it, so your true, unconscious feelings come through.

You can cleanse a place at any time, but naturally it is best done before you move in when the place is empty. Remember to assume your protective bubble (and your 'cloak' if you wish), before starting any cleansing. This bubble has some things in common with the occultist's 'magic circle'.

Arm yourself simply, with a broom or even just a duster. Go into each room in turn, starting upstairs (if there is one), and working your way downwards. Imagine that anything negative is being swept away by broom, or flapped away by duster. Imagine all greyness being driven away, leaving only light, imagine any grumpy entities scuttling off. Sweep all the corners of each room, out through the door, and close the door behind you. In this way, work your way through the house, closing doors as you go. Finally sweep everything out through the front door and close that.

Then place on a tray a joss stick, candle, bowl of salt and bowl of water. If you are used to using incense, you may prefer that to a joss stick. You may like to use some or all scents of copal, benzoin, frankincense, myrrh, sandalwood and vervain. Benzoin, wormwood and myrrh is a strong banishing mixture to use if you really think the place needs a good dose. If so, use the incense as a specific banishing exercise, on its own, and move to a gentler mixture for final cleansing and blessing.

Now go into every room and take each vessel in turn. Sprinkle the salt around saying 'Be blessed by earth', the water with 'Be blessed by water', the joss-stick/incense saying 'Be blessed by air' and the candle saying 'Be blessed by fire'. Then say simply 'Blessed be' and move to the next room. Ask a trusted friend to help you to speed things up! Some people like to seal each doorway with salt and water, also, by sprinkling them all round the openings. It is probably sufficient to do this only with external doorways.

Finally, seal each of the external doors and windows to the house with a protective symbol. My choice would always be the pentagram, or five-point star, and the way to form it is shown in the diagram. You can form it with your forefinger, imagine it appearing as a golden shape in the ether as you stand in front of the door. However, if you are afraid of someone spotting you and thinking you are peculiar, you can make your pentagrams from 'mind-stuff' as you sit inside the house. Imagine each one clearly taking shape in front of each door and window. Do not forget lavatory windows, attic entrances and garage doors. Reinforce your pentagrams every so often and place a large one over the house, for good measure. If you wish, you can place pentagrams at the head and foot of your bed, to protect you while you sleep.

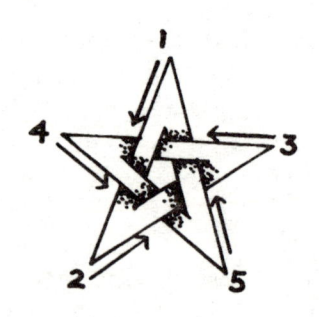

FURTHER READING AND RESOURCES

PUBLICATIONS

P. M. H. Atwater, *Beyond the Light: Near Death Experiences – The Full Story*, Thorsons, 1994

Janet and Colin Bord Diamond, *Modern Mysteries of Britain*, HarperCollins, 1987

Eddie Burks and Gillian Cribbs, *Ghosthunter: Investigating the World of Ghosts and Spirits*, Headline, 1995

T. C. Lethbridge, *Ghost and Ghoul*, Routledge & Kegan Paul, London, 1961

T. C. Lethbridge, *Ghost and Divining Rod*, Routledge & Kegan Paul, London, 1963

David Lorimer, *Survival? Body, Mind and Death in the Light of Psychic Experience*, Routledge & Kegan Paul, London, 1984

Terry White, *The Sceptical Occultist*, Century, 1994

Colin Wilson, *Mysteries*, Grafton, 1986

Colin Wilson, *The Occult*, Grafton, 1989

Relevant and useful titles in this series:

Your Psychic Powers – a beginner's guide, Craig Hamilton-Parker
Mediumship – a beginner's guide, Leo Gough
Witchcraft – a beginner's guide, Teresa Moorey
Shamanism – a beginner's guide, Teresa Moorey
Chakras for beginners, Naomi Ozaniek
Earth Mysteries – a beginner's guide, Teresa Moorey
The Wheel of the Year – Myth and Magic Through the Seasons, Teresa Moorey and Jane Brideson

Psychic News

This weekly paper does its best to verify the credentials of those who advertise. Information also included about America, Canada, South Africa, Australia and New Zealand.

Organisations

The Spiritualist Association of Great Britain
(Mediums will give public demonstrations and can be booked for consultation)
33 Belgrave Square, London SW1X 8QB, UK

The Australian Spiritual Association
PO Box 273, Penrith, NSW 2747, Australia
Tel: (07) 8496450

The Spiritualist Church of Canada
1835 Lawrence Avenue E., Scarborough, Ontario, Canada, M1R 2Y3
Tel: (416) 439-1087

Spiritualist's National Union
Redwoods, Stansted Hall, Stansted, Essex CM24 8UD, UK
Tel: 01279 816363

SNU Centre of Western Australia
579 Murray Street, Perth, 6005, Western Australia

The Institute of Spiritualist Mediums
20 Oakhurst Avenue, East Barnet, Herts EN4 8DL, UK

The College of Psychic Studies
16 Queensberry Place, London SW7 2EB, UK
Tel: 0171 937 8984

The Society for Psychical Research
49 Marloes Road, London W8 6LA, UK

Poltergeist Research Institute
PO Box 118, East Winch, King's Lynn, Norfolk PE32 1ND, UK

The Noah's Ark Society for Physical Mediumship
Newsletter available. Tel: 01263 513067